MASSIVE TRANSFORMATIVE PURPOSE

MASSIVE TRANSFORMATIVE PURPOSE

Index

How was this book written...and why?7
Reflection on capitalism and the future of business,9

Introduction,12
1. **Some definitions of rigor: What is massive transformative purpose (MTP)?14**
    a. Definition and origin of the concept.
    b. The importance of having a MTP in the current context.
    c. How MTP goes beyond traditional mission and vision.
    d. Difference between a normal purpose and a MTP.
2. **The Power of MTP: Global Success Stories,18**
    a. Tesla: Accelerating the transition to sustainable energy.
    b. Google: Organizing the world's information.
    c. Wikipedia: Making all knowledge accessible.
    d. Social movements with MTP: From Greenpeace to Black Lives Matter.
    e. What do these MTPs have in common and why have they been successful?

3. **Why does your organization or project need a MTP?23**
    a. The impact of a MTP on organizational culture.
    b. Attracting talent and clients with purpose.
    c. How MTP builds resilience and adaptability in times of change.
    d. MTP as a driver of innovation.

Part I: Defining Your Massive Transformative Purpose,27

4. **How to identify the core purpose of your organization?28**
    a. Reflection on current values, mission and vision.
    b. Key questions to discover a transformative purpose.
    c. Evaluating the impact, you want to generate in the world.
5. **Criteria for creating a truly transformative MTP,33**
    a. Scalability: What makes a purpose "massive"?
    b. Transformation: How can your MTP change the lives of many people?
    c. Clarity and specificity: Language as a focusing tool.
6. **Practical exercise: creating your massive transformational purpose,38**
    a. Step-by-step guide to defining a MTP.
    b. Brainstorming templates and tools.
    c. Practical examples of MTP in different industries and sectors.

Part II: Implementing and Aligning Your MTP,43

7. **How to align your team and organization around MTP?44**
    a. Purposeful Leadership: How to Inspire Your Team
    b. Communication and storytelling tools to generate cohesion.
    c. Create a purpose-focused organizational culture.
8. **Strategies to incorporate MTP into your business model,49**
    a. How to integrate MTP into your daily operations?
    b. Sustainable and purposeful business models.
    c. Case studies: Companies that have successfully incorporated their MTP into their strategy.
9. **Resistance to change: How to overcome internal challenges, 54**
    a. Identify and manage resistance to change.
    b. Strategies to generate buy-in (support) throughout the organization.

    c. Overcoming cultural and structural barriers.

Part III: Scaling and measuring the impact of your MTP, 59

  10. **How to scale your MTP and maximize global impact? 60**
      a. Tools to scale your purpose.
      b. Using technology and exponential platforms to amplify your MTP.
      c. Examples of organizations that have scaled their impact.

  11. **Measuring the impact of a MTP: Key indicators, 65**
      a. How to measure the success of a MTP? Essential KPIs.
      b. Measure the social, environmental and cultural impact, in addition to the financial impact.
      c. Examples of metrics and tools for tracking results.

  12. **Financing and sustainability of the MTP, 70**
      a. How to finance your long-term purpose?
      b. Impact investments, crowdfunding and other sources.
      c. Success stories of purpose-focused financial models.

Part IV: Inspiration and Community, 77

  13. **Inspiration: Stories of leaders with MTP, 81**
      a. Interviews or inspiring stories from leaders who have implemented a MTP.
      b. Key lessons you can apply to your own transformative purpose.

  14. **Building a global community around your MTP, 85**
      a. How to create a supportive community around your purpose?
      b. Strategies to engage partners, collaborators and consumers.
      c. The power of global movements and collective impact.

  15. **The Future of MTP: How to Evolve with Your Purpose, 90**
      a. Adaptability and evolution of MTP in a constantly changing world.
      b. Anticipation of trends and new opportunities for purpose.
      c. The importance of resilience in the long-term mission.

Conclusion, Summary and Final Reflection, 93
    a. Summary of the key steps to create and implement a MTP.
    b. Final reflection: The potential impact of a MTP on the world.

c. Call to Action: How to start your transformative journey today?

Links

To access related information online:

1. Massive Transformative Purpose Newsletter

   https://www.linkedin.com/newsletters/massive-transformation-purpose-7245782292718055424/

2. Website of Interest: Bencorp Inc.

   https://www.linkedin.com/company/11284218/admin/dashboard/

How was this book written...and why?
by Arturo Benites

It was 2023, I had thought about taking a little break from my company and I was already working for 2 years for technology companies, basically in the banking and commercial industry; one night I suddenly started to feel a tingling, almost anguish, or in any case dissatisfaction, because I was already well into my 40s and thought it was what is very commonly called in my country the mid-life crisis that had been delayed a little; Quite intrigued, I started to think about what the heck was happening to me? So I turned on the TV in the living room and put on the university that we all have at home: YouTube, and I started searching for "something" I honestly didn't know exactly what? And after a long, long, long time I found it: STOICISM.

It was like an awakening for me, a state of rapture something I had experienced before but never at such high levels of Dopamine, over the following days, weeks and months I began to watch many videos of Stoicism, to study its great teachers, such as Marcus Aurelius and Seneca, to understand and practice Stoic philosophy and of course to buy books on Stoicism. Stoicism has led me to a different understanding of life and a reconfiguration of my priorities in it; and that is where we are going with the subject in question, the reason for this book.

For a few years now, I have been thinking about writing, but procrastination always won, with the vain excuses that we all know: I don't have time, I'll do it later, I'll start on vacation, I don't feel motivated now, etc. and blah, blah, blah, so many more. The point here is that, leveraging my recently acquired, new, incipient and hard-learned philosophy, I began to write about a subject that fascinates me, I love it, I could talk for hours and hours without getting tired, I don't know if this has happened to you, it has happened to me twice in my life: with Cosmology - Astronomy and with the Massive Transformative Purpose, both Business and Personal.

Do you see where this is going? Let me tell you a little more, I first studied Massive Transformative Purpose when I was taking a postgraduate course at MIT (Massachusetts Institute of Technology): Leadership in Innovation; and it literally opened my mind, it was a Wow What is this? and I said to myself: this is the best thing I have learned in the last 2 decades; I have to know everything! That is how this story **begins**, this book is about Massive Transformative Purpose in Business, however, it can also be applied to personal life, which I am sure as you have already deduced, yes, I have also applied it to my personal life since I had my pseudo-crisis; but that is another story that I will tell in the next book.

In this book I develop and detail The Massive Transformative Corporate Purpose that I hope more and more companies will follow. If half of them did, it would be something that would change the world and our future. I also leave you with a Reflection on Capitalism and the role that companies have played, the good, the bad and the ugly, like that old movie. So that we can take action on the matter, wake up, get started, act to leave a society with better companies, organizations and institutions that ensure a promising future for our children and the planet.

Reflection on capitalism and the future of business

Capitalism, as we know it today, has been a powerful driver of economic development and technological innovation. Over the centuries, this system has enabled industries to flourish, the creation of wealth, and living conditions to be improved for millions of people. However, it has also led to **growing inequalities**, negative impacts on the environment, and an excessive **focus on short-term profits** rather than long-term well-being. These tensions have led many to question whether traditional capitalism is still adequate to address the challenges of the 21st century or whether it needs a fundamental evolution to confront current problems, such as the climate crisis, social inequality, and financial instability.

Today, more than ever, a new way of thinking about the role of business in society is emerging. Business leaders and academics have begun to explore concepts such as **conscious capitalism**, **stakeholder capitalism**, and **purpose-driven business** as alternatives to the traditional, shareholder-focused capitalist model.

1. Stakeholder capitalism: A necessary change

For decades, shareholder capitalism has dominated the business landscape, prioritizing short-term profits and maximizing shareholder value above all else. However, stakeholder capitalism **proposes** a more inclusive view. Rather than focusing solely on shareholders, this approach advocates for creating value for **all stakeholders**: employees, customers, suppliers, the community, and the environment.

This approach recognizes that businesses do not operate in a vacuum. They are deeply interconnected with their environment and must act responsibly to ensure their own long-term sustainability. As consumer and employee expectations evolve, businesses are forced to rethink their purpose and impact on society.

In this context, companies are beginning to adopt **Massive Transformative Purposes (MTPs)** that go beyond profits and seek a positive impact on society. This shift in focus can be key to the future **legitimacy** of companies, as it allows them to respond to growing social and environmental demands in a way that is beneficial both to society and to their own growth.

2. The rise of purpose-driven companies

The emergence of **purpose-driven companies** has gained momentum in recent years. These companies do not only seek economic profit, but place **social and**

environmental impact at the heart of their business model. A notable example are **B Corps**, which are legally committed to generating a positive social impact while also being financially profitable.

The shift toward purpose-driven businesses reflects a **response to widespread dissatisfaction** with traditional capitalism. More and more people, especially among younger generations, are seeking to align themselves with brands and companies that share their values. For these people, a company's success is not measured solely by its profitability, but also by its ability to positively contribute to the world.

By adopting a MTP, companies can gain not only the loyalty of their customers, but also attract **exceptional talent** looking to work in organizations that have a meaningful purpose. In this sense, MTP can become a driver of innovation, differentiation and long-term competitiveness.

3. The challenge of exponential capitalism and sustainability

The exponential growth of some industries, especially in technology, has accelerated the pace of capitalism and, at the same time, intensified its negative effects. Giant technology companies, such as digital platforms, can create unprecedented wealth, but they can also aggravate problems such as the **concentration of power** and the **unequal distribution of resources**.

As capitalism advances into its most technological and globalized form, questions arise about how to strike a **balance between economic growth and sustainability**. Exponential capitalism poses the challenge that the speed of growth does not always take into account the planet's finite resources. This leads us to consider business models that fully integrate environmental and social concerns – a field in which MTPs can play a crucial role.

Companies of the future will need to address difficult questions about the **use of artificial intelligence**, mass automation, job losses and climate change. And most importantly, they will need to do so in ways that do not just seek economic profit, but also ensure a positive impact on collective well-being.

4. Capitalism and the climate crisis

One of the biggest challenges facing capitalism today is the **climate crisis**. Traditional models of economic growth have failed to take into account environmental costs, leading to the overexploitation of natural resources and an accumulation of irreversible damage to the planet. As the world faces the increasingly evident effects of climate change, businesses have a **critical responsibility** in finding solutions.

The MTP can be a powerful framework for businesses to take a proactive role in tackling climate change. By establishing a purpose that not only drives economic growth but also addresses global challenges such as environmental sustainability, companies can be an active part of the solution. Initiatives such as the transition to renewable energy, carbon reduction and the circular economy are areas where companies can lead and make a real impact.

5. The future of business: Adaptability and purpose

The future of capitalism and business is not set in stone. The key will be the ability of organizations to **adapt to new** social realities and expectations. Rather than resisting change, companies that embrace more **inclusive, responsible and sustainable business models** will have a greater chance of thriving.

MTP provides a framework for this evolution. By focusing on a purpose larger than just economic growth, companies not only prepare to meet the challenges of the future, but also inspire employees, consumers and investors to join their mission.

Ultimately, the future of capitalism may not be a trade-off between profit or purpose. Companies that manage to integrate both concepts coherently and strategically will be the ones leading the way towards a **more human capitalism** – one that generates value for all stakeholders, while creating a positive impact on society and the planet.

Conclusion: A capitalism with purpose

Capitalism is at a **tipping point**. As businesses face increasing pressures to be more responsible, sustainable, and fair, the path to long-term success is closely tied to their ability to embrace a **Massive Transformative Purpose**. MTP is not only a tool for social change, but it is also a viable strategy for business sustainability in the future.

Today's entrepreneurs have the opportunity to **redefine capitalism**, moving it toward a more inclusive and conscious model, where purpose and positive impact are as important as profits. The result will be an economic system that works better for everyone, where businesses not only thrive, but also help create a better world.

And as the great master Dale Carnegie said:

"This is an action book."

Let's get started...

Introduction

The biggest problem I've encountered and set out for this book to solve is **how to move from an inspiring, massive vision to concrete, scalable, measurable execution**. It should help people and organizations clearly define their Massive Transformative Purpose, align it with their capabilities and resources, and create a practical roadmap that enables them to achieve transformative impact at scale.

I clearly see 3 major problems, and if I repeat: problems, first things should be called by their name, as they are, not with euphemisms, such as challenge, challenging, or very challenging challenge, which is nothing other than saying: unrealistic many times. In my experience people tend to overestimate themselves much more than underestimate themselves and to make the problem worse there is often a huge gap between the commercial team that approves a project and the operations team that executes it. Example: Real life case, an ACME bank had a very important, vital, strategic project, and they made a classic estimate of time, budget and quality, as good project management indicates, so far so good, the problem lies in that the development and implementation time that was supposed to be 2 years was put at 9 months! Yes, you read that right, my dear reader, less than half the time needed for it to turn out well, that is, without exceeding the budget and with the expected quality standards... Then they sell it to you, your "leaders" or rather bosses as a challenging and very demanding project, translation: Unreal, impossible to achieve with the parameters described. And then when the problems arise that we already know are going to arise, well, guess who do you think they blame? Which team is responsible? Where do they look for the guilty ones? Normally in the team that executes the project, I have never, ever, unfortunately in my 25 years of experience, seen it be any other way. Second, another of the main "challenges", I repeat **problems**, is balancing the immediate needs of the business with the long-term vision. Often, there is a pressure to deliver quick results, here is a short example: Imagine a Payment Processing Solutions company like ACME, there are now all over the world, which places the famous POS (Point of Sale) to their clients, here is the problem: The IT Manager together with the Commercial Manager and their respective teams have the goal (provided by the company's Management) of closing the year with 500K POS placed in the city; however, this short-term goal goes in direct contrast with what the Architecture Manager and the MTP Consultant have developed, because for them the long-term goal of getting 50% of the market (let's say 6 million POS placed in 3 years) is more important than this short-term goal and I insist, unfortunately the projects that involve achieving the short-term goal of 500K and the long-term goal of 6MM are not compatible. So, what do we do? It is clear that the long-term goal is the most profitable for the company (this conclusion is provided in a report to the Management by the Architecture Manager and the MTP Consultant) and it is the logical and intelligent way to follow, however there is the problem that the short-term goal given to the IT and Commercial teams is already in process, that is, there will be rework to do that involves corrections, changes, etc. And also, what happens with the bonus? Yes, the bonus for meeting goals promised to the IT and Commercial teams, well it is evident that they are not going to meet the goal, and another thing, the Financial Manager. Will he agree with this solution? Well it is clear that the company will receive less income this year and will not meet its goal either. As you can see, there are many and big problems here and many of them do not have to do directly with the <u>Solution itself</u>, but with the people, because you always have to keep in mind the employees, collaborators, the people; it is not always about functions, architecture, MTP, etc. you always have to analyze and take people into account. And last but not least, as a third problem, there is the issue of managing resistance to change (chapter 9 detail) since the business transformation that can often be part of a MTP involves redefining processes and roles. This problem must also be seen from the point of view of people as it can generate concern among employees.

So how do we begin? Well, I turned to the master Ryan Holiday for help, and in his book "Courage is Calling" he clearly expresses what is needed, what an organization needs from its leaders and I quote: "Courage is contagious... <<one man with courage makes a majority>>... When you are brave, you change reality because by doing so you make others brave. Like a virus, serenity is transmitted by contact. It is transmitted through the air. We exude it, we give others the strength we have left over and we infect them as they infect others, not with a degrading and harmful agent, but with one that develops strength and purpose."

That's right, colleagues, COURAGE, the first thing is leadership with courage, it is an excellent start, one of the 4 stoic virtues.

Chapter 1: Some rigorous definitions: What is Massive Transformative Purpose (MTP)?

Massive Transformative Purpose (MTP) is an idea that has gained relevance in recent years due to the growing need for organizations, companies, and social movements to find a reason for being beyond financial objectives or the satisfaction of immediate needs. In this first chapter, we will explore in depth the meaning of MTP, its conceptual roots, why it is essential in the current context, and how it differs from other concepts such as mission, vision, or values.

1.1 Definition and origin of the concept

Massive Transformative Purpose was popularized by **Salim Ismail**, founder of **Singularity University,** in his book Exponential Organizations. The concept is closely linked to organizations and individuals who do not simply seek economic growth or business success, but aspire to have a **large-scale positive impact** on society.

A MTP is a statement of purpose that:

a. **Inspire transformation** in the world or an industry.
b. **Seeks to solve a problem or take advantage of an opportunity** in a radical and exponential way.
c. **It affects a large number of people** (millions or even billions).

Example of MTP definition:

a. Tesla: "Accelerating the world's transition to sustainable energy."
b. Google: "Organizing the world's information and making it universally accessible and useful."
c. Bencorp Inc.: "Our business is helping today's businessmen and leaders create a better tomorrow."

In short, a MTP is a bold, inspiring, change-oriented goal that guides an organization or movement's strategic approach toward creating massive, transformative impact.

Key features of MTP:

1. **Scalability:** MTP has the potential to influence and impact millions of people.
2. **Transformation:** It is not just about improving a system or a process, but about **radically changing the way things are done.**
3. **Positive purpose:** It is oriented towards a greater good that goes beyond economic benefits.

1.2 The importance of MTP in the current context

We live in a world that is experiencing rapid and significant changes due to factors such as technology, globalization, climate change and social crises. These changes bring with them both challenges and opportunities. To stay relevant, organizations must not only adapt but **lead** these changes through innovation and a clear purpose.

In this context, a MTP is crucial because:

   a. **Inspire teams and audiences:** A transformative purpose mobilizes both employees and customers, generating a sense of belonging and contribution to something bigger.
   b. **Fosters resilience:** Organizations that operate with a MTP have a greater capacity to adapt and evolve in the face of crises and disruptions.
   c. **Attract and retain talent:** New generations of employees, particularly Millennials and Generation Z, are looking to work for organizations that have a positive impact on the world. A MTP attracts these professionals.
   d. **Drive innovation:** Organizations with a clear purpose are more innovative, as they are constantly looking for solutions that enable them to achieve their transformative goals.

Technological and social context

Technology has enabled organizations with MTP to scale faster than ever before. Digital platforms, artificial intelligence, and exponential technologies enable organizations **to amplify their impact** and reach more people, at a speed never seen before. For example, companies like Uber or Airbnb have managed to transform their industries thanks to technologies that accelerate exponential growth.

On the other hand, the social environment is also changing. Today, consumers prefer to support brands that **share their values** and are committed to solving social problems, such as inequality, climate change or community well-being. A MTP allows organizations to align themselves with these new social expectations.

1.3 Why does it go beyond the traditional mission and vision?

Although many confuse MTP with the concepts of **mission and vision,** it is important to note that MTP goes beyond these traditional ideas. While mission and vision are statements that define what a company does and where it wants to go, MTP is a statement that **involves the entire organization** in a **much bolder and more transformative mission,** which exceeds operational and financial limits.

Key differences:

a. **Mission:** Describes what the company does or what it seeks to achieve in the short or medium term.
b. **Vision:** Defines where the organization wants to go in the future.
c. **MTP:** It is an inspiring, massive, long-term statement that is aimed at profoundly transforming an industry, a community or the world.

The MTP doesn't just set a direction, it **drives change.** For example, while an energy company may have a mission to provide electricity to its customers, a MTP in that context would be something like "make the world 100% reliant on clean, renewable energy." This type of purpose mobilizes more people and amplifies impact.

1.4 Difference between a common purpose and a MTP

A common purpose is often focused on meeting a company's internal or immediate needs, such as generating profits, improving customer satisfaction, or growing its industry. A MTP, however, focuses on **changing the rules of the game,** by offering a disruptive solution to a global problem or substantially improving people's lives on a massive scale.

Comparison between common purpose and MTP:

a. **Common purpose:** "To offer high quality products to our customers."
b. **MTP:** "Making every home in the world energy self-sufficient."

A MTP is not content with doing things well or being competitive; it seeks a **transformative impact** that resonates with millions of people and the planet itself.

Conclusion

Massive Transformative Purpose is a powerful tool that enables organizations, movements, and individuals to lead massive, positive change in the world. It goes beyond traditional concepts of mission and vision, setting a bold, scalable direction that not only transforms an industry or sector, but **inspires people and mobilizes resources** to achieve long-term impact.

This chapter has laid the groundwork for understanding what a MTP is, why it is essential in today's context, and how it differs from other strategic leadership concepts. In the next chapters, we will delve deeper into how organizations can **define, implement, and scale** their own MTP, and how this strategy can radically change both a company's internal focus and its impact on the world.

Chapter 2: The Power of MTP: Global Success Stories

A **Massive Transformative Purpose (MTP)** is not just an aspirational statement, but a powerful force for change that has enabled companies, organizations, and social movements **to change the course of history.** In this chapter, we will explore examples of how MTP has been successfully implemented, highlighting both companies and global movements that have managed to transform industries, societies, and even the way we live.

2.1 Why is it important to learn from examples?

Throughout recent history, many of the most profound changes in society have been driven by people and organizations with a clear purpose. Learning from these examples allows us to understand not only **what a successful MTP is,** but also **how it can be applied** in different contexts.

Benefits of studying MTP examples:

a. **Inspire:** By seeing how others have made great changes, readers can see the possibility of doing the same in their own industries or communities.
b. **They offer a map:** These examples offer a model of **best practices** that can be adapted or replicated.
c. **Demonstrate impact:** They show how a MTP can lead to concrete results, both in terms of innovation and social or economic change.

2.2 Business examples of MTP

Tesla: Accelerating the world's transition to sustainable energy

Tesla MTP: "Accelerating the world's transition to sustainable energy."

Background: Founded by Elon Musk, Tesla is not just an electric car company; it is a **purpose-driven, transformative organization** that seeks to reduce the world's dependence on fossil fuels and accelerate the use of renewable energy.

Impact:

a. **Disruptive innovation:** Tesla changed the global perception of electric vehicles, proving that they could be **luxurious, fast and efficient.** It has also driven the transition towards a more sustainable transport system.

b. **Scalability:** It doesn't just limit itself to making cars, it has also invested in technologies such as **batteries** and large-scale energy storage systems, helping to transform energy supply around the world.
   c. **Overall result:** Tesla has influenced other major automotive brands to follow suit and develop their own lines of electric cars, accelerating the global transformation of the transportation industry.

Google: Organizing the world's information and making it universally accessible

Google MTP: "Organizing the world's information and making it universally accessible and useful."

Background: Founded by Larry Page and Sergey Brin, Google began not simply as a search engine, but as a company with the massive purpose of **organizing human knowledge** and making it accessible to everyone.

Impact:
   a. **Transforming access to information:** Google has revolutionized how people access and use information around the world. From search to tools like Google Maps, Gmail, and Google Scholar, the company has made access to information almost instantaneous.
   b. **Scalability and global relevance:** Google now has billions of users around the world, and its mission continues to expand with new technologies like artificial intelligence (AI), **Google Translate**, and other educational platforms.
   c. **Overall outcome:** The democratization of information has enabled people to learn, research and collaborate at an unprecedented level, reducing knowledge barriers.

Wikipedia: Making all knowledge accessible

Wikipedia MTP: "Empowering and engaging people around the world to collect and develop educational content under a free license."

Context: Wikipedia, founded by Jimmy Wales and Larry Sanger, was born as a collaborative project to make human knowledge **freely available** to anyone with Internet access.

Impact:
   a. **Mass Participation:** Wikipedia is a perfect example of how a transformative purpose can **empower millions of people** to collaborate on a common project. Anyone can contribute to the platform, which has enabled the creation of the world's largest encyclopedia.

> b. **Global impact**: With over 300 languages available and millions of articles, Wikipedia has radically changed the way we access knowledge, making it **free and accessible** to anyone.
> c. **Overall outcome**: Wikipedia has democratized access to knowledge, allowing individuals around the world to participate in building a shared knowledge base.

2.3 Examples of social movements with MTP

Greenpeace: Defending the global environment

Greenpeace MTP: "Defending the environment worldwide and promoting green solutions to ensure a sustainable future."

Background: Founded in 1971, Greenpeace is a global organization dedicated to protecting the environment by advocating sustainable practices and opposing the exploitation of natural resources.

Impact:

> a. **Change in environmental policies**: Greenpeace has influenced environmental legislation globally, pressuring governments and corporations to adopt more sustainable practices.
> b. **Mass mobilization**: Greenpeace has mobilized millions of people around the world, raising awareness about problems such as deforestation, whaling, and climate change.
> c. **Overall results**: The organization has been key in promoting **environmental activism** at a global level, achieving changes in company and government policies.

Black Lives Matter: Transforming Racial Justice

Black Lives Matter MTP: "Eradicate white supremacy and build local power to intervene in the violence inflicted on Black communities by the state and vigilantes."

Background: Founded in 2013 by Patrisse Cullors, Alicia Garza, and Opal Tometi, Black Lives Matter (BLM) is an international movement fighting against systemic violence and inequality toward black people.

Impact:

> a. **Global awareness on racism**: Through mass protests and social media campaigns, BLM has transformed the global conversation on racial justice.

b. **Scalability**: Although it began in the United States, the movement has spread to countries around the world, prompting policy changes and police reforms in several nations.
c. **Overall outcome**: BLM has brought about concrete changes to laws, policies and systems that perpetuate racial inequality, and has inspired millions to take part in the fight against discrimination.

2.4 What do these MTPs have in common?

While the examples above span different sectors, from technology to social activism, all of these MTPs have some key features in common:

1. **They are ambitious and bold**: They are not satisfied with incremental improvements; they seek **radical transformations** that change the world.
2. **They have a global impact**: These MTPs have the capacity to affect millions or billions of people, whether through technology, access to information or social mobilization.
3. **They are inspiring**: Successful MTPs inspire their audiences, whether employees, customers, users or activists, to join their cause.
4. **They are sustainable**: Well-designed MTPs focus on **long-lasting solutions**, which continue to evolve and adapt as global conditions change.
5. **Mobilizing the community**: A successful MTP is not just about the organization leading it; it mobilizes ordinary people to contribute and feel part of the transformation.

Conclusion

The examples of **Massive Transformative Purposes** we've explored in this chapter demonstrate the power of a bold purpose to change industries, societies, and even global culture. Tesla, Google, Wikipedia, Greenpeace, and Black Lives Matter have all achieved results that transcend what one company or movement might expect, thanks to their focus on radical transformation and their ability to mobilize millions of people toward a common good.

In the next chapters, we will explore how you can apply the principles of MTP to your own organization or project, and what steps to take to design a purpose that truly transforms your environment and the world.

Chapter 3: Why does your organization or project need a MTP?

In this chapter we will delve into the key aspects that explain why a Massive Transformative Purpose (MTP) is not just an idealistic statement, but a fundamental driver for the sustainable success of any organization. We will see how it directly impacts **organizational culture**, how it can attract purpose-driven talent and customers, how it generates **resilience** in times of uncertainty, and finally, how it acts as a **driver of innovation**.

3.1 The Impact of a MTP on Organizational Culture

A MTP has the power to transform **organizational culture** by providing a shared reason for being for every member of the organization. This greater purpose acts as a compass that guides behaviors, decisions, and relationships within the company.

3.1.1 Building a Purpose-Centered Culture

- **Values alignment**: When an organization adopts a MTP, the values that underpin it are reflected in every aspect of internal operations. This makes it easier for every employee, regardless of level, to understand how their daily work contributes to a larger impact.

- **Motivation and Engagement**: Employees who feel they are working toward a transformative goal experience greater motivation and job satisfaction. Research shows that people who believe their work has a purpose beyond financial gain are **3 times more likely to be engaged** and productive in their work.

- **Collaboration and empowerment**: A MTP also fosters a culture of collaboration. When employees feel part of a larger mission, they tend to collaborate more effectively, feel empowered to make decisions aligned with that purpose, and take greater responsibility for their results.

3.1.2 Purpose and sense of community

A MTP creates a **sense of community** among employees as they are not just working for a company, but to improve the world in some capacity. This mindset strengthens internal bonds and makes people feel united by a common cause, which also decreases employee turnover and improves the work environment.

3.2 Attracting talent and customers with purpose

A well-defined MTP not only impacts internally, but also has a powerful effect on **attracting talent and clients**. More and more people are looking for more than just a salary or a product; they are looking for a connection with organizations that have a deep purpose and a positive impact on the world.

3.2.1 Attracting Talent with Purpose

- **Employees looking for more than just a job**: Employees, especially those from new generations like **millennials and Gen Z**, want to be part of something bigger than themselves. They are looking for employers who share their values and offer purpose in everyday work.
- **Competition in the labor market**: In a highly competitive labor market, companies with a strong MTP have a significant advantage. Not only do they attract top talent, but those employees also tend to be more **loyal** and **productive**, as they feel a greater emotional connection to their work.
- **Talent retention: A LinkedIn** study found that purpose-driven companies reduce their turnover rate by up to **40%**. Purpose transforms work into a shared mission, which increases employee loyalty.

3.2.2 Customer attraction and loyalty

Modern customers are looking for brands that align with their values. A strong MTP builds trust and loyalty in consumers as they are **not just looking to buy products or services, but to be part of a mission**. Companies with a clear MTP like **TOMS**, which donates a pair of shoes for every pair purchased, or **Patagonia**, which prioritizes environmental sustainability, have cultivated deep and lasting relationships with their customers thanks to their purpose-driven approach.

- **Emotional connection**: Consumers tend to create an emotional bond with brands that they feel are making a difference. This translates into higher **lifetime value** and a greater willingness to recommend the brand.
- **Customers as ambassadors**: Customers who identify with an organization's MTP become its **best ambassadors**, sharing their experience and promoting the brand organically.

3.3 How MTP builds resilience and adaptability in times of change

A strong MTP not only provides direction in good times, but also offers **resilience** and adaptability during times of crisis or uncertainty. Having a deep purpose guiding the organization helps keep the course when circumstances are difficult.

3.3.1 Focus on the long term

Organizations with a MTP think **long-term**, which allows them to act calmly and decisively in times of adversity. This approach helps them:

- **Making strategic decisions**: Rather than reacting impulsively to crises, a MTP enables decisions to be made that are aligned with the organization's core values, thereby protecting its long-term vision.
- **Maintaining team engagement**: During difficult situations, employees who are aligned with a MTP have a greater ability to withstand pressure. This is because they understand that their work has meaning beyond the immediate survival of the organization.

3.3.2 Adaptation and agility

A MTP also fosters an agile and adaptable mindset. Companies with a higher purpose are better able to adjust their operations and approaches without losing sight of their core mission. This translates into:

- **Innovation capacity**: Organizations guided by a MTP tend to be more innovative in times of change, as their purpose allows them to identify new opportunities to achieve their transformative vision.
- **Organizational resilience**: According to the **Boston Consulting Group**, companies that operate with a clear purpose are 20% more likely to overcome an economic recession or global crisis, because their purpose connects them emotionally with all their stakeholders.

3.4 The MTP as a driver of innovation

A Massive Transformative Purpose not only guides the organization, but also serves as a **driver of innovation**. A Massive Transformative Purpose forces companies to think beyond conventional solutions and look for innovative ways to fulfill their mission.

3.4.1 Purpose-led innovation

Companies with a MTP are not content with incremental improvement of their products or services. They are driven to create **massive impact**, and to do so, they must constantly innovate. MTP inspires teams to question the status quo, seek new ways of doing things, and generate disruptive solutions.

Example: **Tesla**. Its MVP, "accelerating the world's transition to sustainable energy," has fueled the creation of electric vehicles, solar power systems, and battery storage that are revolutionizing entire industries.

3.4.2 Collaborative innovation

MTP also fosters **collaborative innovation** by bringing together different departments and strategic partners under a single vision. Teams that would normally operate in silos are encouraged to work together to achieve the transformative goal, leading to greater synergy and creativity.

- **Drive towards new technologies**: Organizations with a MTP are motivated to adopt and even develop new technologies that help them fulfill their mission, allowing them to be at the forefront of industrial innovation.

Conclusion

A Massive Transformative Purpose profoundly transforms the way an organization operates. From **internal culture** to the ability to attract and retain talent and customers, to its ability to adapt and innovate, a Massive Transformative Purpose establishes a solid foundation for long-term success. Today's business world is no longer focused solely on economic growth, but on the social and environmental impact an organization can generate. For companies looking to lead into the future, embracing a Massive Transformative Purpose is not just an option, it's a necessity.

In the next chapter, we'll dive into **how to define your MTP**, with a step-by-step guide to creating a purpose that resonates both internally and externally.

Part I: Defining Your Massive Transformative Purpose

The great teacher Viktor Frankl, whom I greatly respect, in his book "Man's Search for Meaning" explains the meaning of life and how it can be discovered in three ways, and I quote: "(1) by performing an action; (2) by accepting the gifts of existence; (3) by suffering."

He also defines with extreme clarity and subtlety something he called: The Essence of existence and the primary concern of man, let me explain: The essence of existence defines it and I quote: "it consists of the capacity of the human being to respond responsibly to the demands that life presents in each particular situation" … "the primary concern of man is not to enjoy pleasure, or avoid pain, but to find a meaning to life."

Are you connecting the dots yet? Doesn't "Finding meaning in life" sound similar to what we might call "Finding your purpose in life"? So, applied to your personal life, in my experience, Viktor Frankl's teachings are extremely useful, reliable and unquestionable. Now, if we think a little more, how would it be to apply it to companies, organizations, institutions? After all, these are constituted, directed and led by people; that is, we find a way for people, in this case businessmen, entrepreneurs, and leaders, to have the courage necessary to exude it to them… hmm, exactly! As Michael Jackson said: "This is It." That's it: Massive Transformative Purpose!

Chapter 4: How to identify the core purpose of your organization?

A **Massive Transformative Purpose (MTP)** must be deeply aligned with the core of your organization. To identify this purpose, it is essential to introspect on your current values, mission, and vision, as well as reflect on the impact you want to make in the world. This chapter offers a guide to discovering that core purpose and making it the driving force of your project or organization.

4.1 Reflection on current values, mission and vision

The first step in identifying MTP is to review and analyze your organization's current **values**, **mission,** and **vision**. These three key pieces are the foundation of your organization and determine its reason for being.

4.1.1 Evaluation of current values

Values are the beliefs and principles that guide behavior within the organization. To identify an authentic MTP, it is crucial that these values are strong and reflected in the company's daily actions.

- **Questions to reflect on values**:
    - What do we value most as an organization?
    - How do our values influence decision-making?
    - Are these values aligned with the impact we want to have on the world?

If you find that your current values are not strong enough or aligned with a greater purpose, it may be necessary to reframe them to be more in tune with the transformative mission you seek.

4.1.2 Mission review

The mission should be the starting point for defining a MTP, but many times this statement focuses too much on the present and operational aspects.

- **Questions to reflect on the mission**:
    - Does our current mission reflect a transformative intention?
    - How does our mission relate to large-scale positive change?
    - Is our mission inspiring enough to mobilize employees, customers and partners?

Often, organizations find that their mission is functional, but not ambitious. This is where the need to take that mission to the next level comes in: massive transformation.

4.1.3 Vision review

A **vision** is a statement of the future that the organization wants to create. A MTP must be deeply aligned with this vision while simultaneously pushing the boundaries of what is possible.

- **Questions to reflect on the vision**:
    - Is our vision bold enough?
    - Does our vision project a positive change that will impact not only the organization, but also the world?
    - Is our vision clear and emotionally powerful enough to inspire in the long term?

The vision must be ambitious, but also clear and realistic in its ability to inspire the entire organization to work towards it.

4.2 Key questions to discover a transformative purpose

Identifying a transformational purpose requires a process of deep reflection that goes beyond business objectives. Here are a series of **key questions** that will help you discover a transformative purpose.

4.2.1 What global or social problem do you want to help solve?

A MTP is usually related to a large global or **societal problem that the organization is seeking to solve. The essential question here is: What is the big challenge that you want to help solve?**

- **Example**: If you're in tech, the issue might be bridging the digital divide in marginalized communities or promoting global access to digital education.
- **Reflection**: Purpose should go beyond the immediate interests of the company and focus on something that has a lasting positive impact on society.

4.2.2 How can your organization generate meaningful change?

It is important to reflect on **how your organization** is equipped to address the identified global problem. Do you have the resources, knowledge or capacity to create real change?

- **Example**: If you are a food company, can you contribute to fighting hunger or improving sustainability in the food supply chain?
- **Reflection**: The purpose must be aligned with your organizational strengths and capabilities, which will increase your chances of success.

4.2.3 What will inspire your employees and customers to join your cause?

A MTP should not only be relevant, but also **inspiring**. It should excite and engage both employees and customers, motivating them to be part of the change.

- **Example**: How can you connect your MTP to your employees' passions and interests? What message will resonate with your customers and turn them into advocates for your mission?
- **Reflection**: The MTP should be something that inspires people to actively participate in its execution, generating a feeling of shared purpose.

4.2.4 What will never change in your organization?

An important question in defining a MTP is to identify what is fundamental and **unchangeable** in your organization. This is the core of the purpose, what will guide the company over time, regardless of market or industry changes.

- **Example**: In a technology company, it may be a commitment to innovation. In an NGO, it could be improving the quality of life in vulnerable communities.
- **Reflection**: Defining what will never change will help you identify the very essence of MTP.

4.3 Evaluating the impact you want to generate in the world

A crucial part of defining a MTP is understanding the **impact** you want to create over the long term. These are not just vague aspirations, but **concrete, measurable goals** that reflect your commitment to transformation.

4.3.1 Define the long-term impact

To define a solid MTP, it is essential to think long-term. Ask yourself what impact you expect your organization to have in the coming decades.

- **Example**: If your MTP is related to environmental sustainability, do you expect to reduce carbon emissions from your operations? Will you contribute to global reforestation or the development of renewable energy?
- **Reflection**: Long-term impact should be ambitious and tangible, something your organization can measure and consistently progress toward.

4.3.2 How do we measure the success of your MTP?

Defining how the success of your MTP will be measured is essential to ensure that your purpose is translated into real action and not just words. Establishing **key performance indicators (KPIs)** to measure your progress towards the desired impact is a critical step.

- **Example**: If your MTP is geared toward improving education, you could measure success by the number of students you have provided access to quality educational tools or by reducing the gender gap in education in vulnerable communities.
- **Reflection**: Having clear metrics will not only help you stay focused, but will also be a way to demonstrate the real impact of your MTP to your employees, customers and stakeholders.

4.3.3 How to ensure your impact is sustainable?

A MTP must be designed to be **sustainable over the long term**. It is not just about creating an immediate impact, but about ensuring that the changes generated endure and continue to improve the world over time.

- **Example**: If your MTP focuses on reducing resource waste, how will you ensure that the implemented changes are maintained even after the business grows or market conditions change?
- **Reflection**: MTP sustainability involves a commitment to positive impact over time, and is vital to the authenticity and effectiveness of the purpose.

Conclusion

Discovering your organization's **Massive Transformative Purpose** is a deep process that requires honest reflection on your current values, mission, and vision, as well as a detailed analysis of the impact you want to make in the world. By answering key questions and assessing both your internal capabilities and your long-term aspirations, you will be able to identify a Massive Transformative Purpose that inspires your organization, attracts talent and customers, and positions your company as a transformative force in society.

In the next chapter, we'll look at how to **implement your MTP**, aligning it with your organization's culture and daily operations so that it becomes a real force for change.

Chapter 5: Criteria for creating a truly transformative MTP

Defining a **Massive Transformative Purpose (MTP)** is not simply a matter of choosing an inspiring statement. For it to be truly transformative, it must meet certain criteria that allow it to not only resonate on a conceptual level, but also generate real, massive impact. In this chapter, we will explore the three key pillars that every MTP must have: **scalability**, **transformation**, and **clarity**.

5.1 Scalability: What makes a purpose "massive"?

The concept of "massiveness" in a MTP refers to its ability to **scale** and generate an impact that transcends borders, affecting not only a small group, but many people in different contexts. A purpose is massive when it has the potential to **replicate** and **grow**, influencing sectors or communities far beyond its origin.

5.1.1 Global or systemic scope

For a purpose to be truly massive, it must have the potential to be **global or systemic**. This means that your MTP must be able to address a problem that, ideally, affects a large portion of the world's population, or a fundamental aspect of an economic, social or environmental system.

- **Example: Google** 's mission to "organize the world's information and make it universally accessible and useful" is on a massive scale because it addresses a challenge that affects virtually every human being: access to information.
- **Reflection**: Consider how your organization can impact not only its immediate market or community, but also a much broader audience. Ask yourself if the problem you are trying to solve has the potential for global scalability or if you can develop a replicable model in different contexts.

5.1.2 Replicability and growth

A MTP must be **replicable**, meaning that the impact it creates can extend beyond a single instance or community. Replicability allows your purpose to expand and grow without being limited by geographic, economic, or social barriers.

- **Example**: **TED** is another example of a scalable MTP. Its motto "ideas worth spreading" reflects a massive purpose that has been replicated globally through TEDx events in thousands of communities around the world.
- **Reflection**: Consider whether your MTP has the potential to scale. How can you build a model that allows your mission and impact to extend into new

areas or communities? What resources, platforms, or networks will you need to facilitate that growth?

5.1.3 Technology and resources

Technology plays a crucial role in the scalability of a MTP. Technology enables the rapid dissemination of information, **the** creation of collaborative networks, and the implementation of solutions at scale. A scalable MTP must consider how to leverage emerging technologies to amplify its impact.

- **Example**: **Tesla** and its mission to accelerate the world's transition to sustainable energy has scaled through the use of technology. Its advances in batteries, solar energy and electric vehicles have been key to its ability to make a global impact.
- **Reflection**: Think about how you can integrate technologies, digital platforms or innovative models that allow your MTP to grow exponentially. Technology is not only an enabler, but a key tool to massify the impact of your purpose.

5.2 Transformation: How can your MTP change the lives of many people?

For a purpose to be truly transformative, it must have the power to **change lives**. An effective MTP generates a tangible and meaningful impact on people's lives, improving their well-being, opportunities or quality of life in a visible and lasting way.

5.2.1 Significant and tangible impact

The MTP must offer a solution that **solves a significant problem** and transforms the daily experience of those it affects. This impact must be perceptible and significant, generating a change that people can directly feel.

- **Example: Airbnb** 's MTP — "creating a world where anyone can belong anywhere" — not only changed the way we travel, but also how we experience hospitality and community. This transformation has been tangible for millions of travelers and hosts around the world.
- **Reflection**: Reflect on how your MTP tangibly impacts people. Ask yourself: How will it improve the lives of individuals or communities? What personal or social transformation can it generate in the short, medium and long term?

5.2.2 Changing systems and paradigms

A MTP must not only transform individuals, but also contribute to changing broader **systems and paradigms. This means that it must challenge existing norms and structures to create a new order that benefits a greater number of people.**

- **Example: Patagonia** 's MTP, focused on saving the planet, has transformed not only its customers, but also the fashion industry. By advocating for sustainable practices and promoting responsible consumption, Patagonia has initiated a change in an entire sector.
- **Reflection**: Consider how your MTP can change not just at an individual level, but also structurally. Can you redesign an industry, system, or paradigm to be more fair, efficient, or sustainable? A truly transformative MTP must create changes that affect entire systems.

5.2.3 Generation of opportunities

Part of the transformation brought about by a MTP is the **creation of new opportunities** for those who have traditionally been marginalized or excluded. This may include employment opportunities, education, access to resources or improved living conditions.

- **Example**: **One Laptop per Child** is an example of a MTP that seeks to transform global education by providing children in underprivileged communities with access to educational technology. This MTP has created educational opportunities for millions of children around the world.
- **Reflection**: Reflect on how your MTP can create new opportunities for those who need it most. How can you empower people to improve their lives and create positive change through your mission?

5.3 Clarity and specificity: Language as a focusing tool

Clarity and **specificity** in language are essential to making a MTP understandable, inspiring and actionable. A purpose that is confusing or too vague loses its ability to inspire others and **mobilize** resources. How you articulate your MTP is key to its success.

5.3.1 Clear and concise language

The purpose must be expressed in clear, simple and understandable terms for everyone. A successful MTP is easy to remember, easy to share and easy to understand by anyone, from an employee to a customer or investor.

- **Example: SpaceX** 's MTP, "making life multi-planetary," is extremely clear and direct. There is no ambiguity in their mission, allowing all team members and their supporters to understand exactly what they want to achieve.
- **Reflection**: Make sure your MTP is expressed clearly and concisely. Avoid jargon or vague statements. A good MTP should be easy to share and understand in one powerful sentence.

5.3.2 Focus and specificity

A MTP should be focused on a **specific transformation**. While its impact may be broad, the purpose should be centered on a concrete change and directed toward a specific target group or problem.

- **Example**: **Charity: Water**, whose purpose is to "bring clean, safe drinking water to people in developing countries," is a perfect example of a specific, focused MTP. It addresses a clear problem (lack of access to clean water) with a defined, measurable solution.
- **Reflection**: Review your MTP and ask yourself if it is specific enough. Are you trying to cover too many topics or issues? A more specific MTP is easier to execute and, at the same time, communicate effectively.

5.3.3 The power of words

The **language** you use in your MTP should not only be clear, but also **emotionally powerful**. Words have the power to inspire, mobilize, and create an emotional connection with your audience. A good MTP should generate an emotional response and a sense of urgency or passion for the cause.

- **Example: The Body Shop** 's MTP, "enrich rather than exploit," uses strong, emotional language that not only communicates its mission, but generates a visceral response in those who identify with its values.
- **Reflection**: Consider the words you are using in your MTP. Are they powerful enough to generate an emotional reaction? See how you can adjust the language to inspire and move those who read it.

Conclusion

A truly effective and sustainable **Massive Transformative Purpose** must meet key criteria: **scalability**, **transformation**, and **clarity**. These principles ensure that your MTP is not only ambitious, but also executable and capable of generating real impact on people's lives and systems.

When designing your MTP, make sure it has the potential to scale globally, transform lives in meaningful ways, and be clearly understood by everyone involved. By following these criteria, you can create a MTP that not only inspires, but truly transforms the world.

Chapter 6: Practical Exercise: Creating Your Massive Transformative Purpose

This chapter is designed to guide you step-by-step through the creation of your own **Massive Transformative Purpose (MTP)**. Through practical exercises, templates, and examples, you will be able to define a clear, scalable purpose that is aligned with the values of your organization or project. As you follow this guide, you will discover how to formulate a MTP that inspires, mobilizes, and generates real impact in your sector or community.

6.1 Step-by-step guide to defining a MTP

Below is a detailed process for developing a solid MTP. Follow these steps sequentially to arrive at a purpose statement that is transformative and massive.

Step 1: Reflect on your mission, vision and values

To begin creating a MTP, it is essential that you have clarity about your organization's **mission, vision, and values. Your MTP must be aligned with these core principles.**

- **Mission**: What is your organization's purpose? What fundamental problem are you trying to solve?
- **Vision**: How do you envision the future if your organization succeeds in achieving its mission on a large scale?
- **Values**: What are the core principles that guide your organization and that you want to be reflected in your MTP?

    Exercise: Briefly outline your organization's mission, vision, and core values. Reflect on how these principles can be scaled up to have a transformative impact.

Step 2: Identify the global problem you want to solve

A successful MTP addresses a **global or systemic problem** that affects many people. This is the most important step, as the purpose must be something that truly resonates with your audience.

- Key Question: What is the biggest challenge facing your industry, sector or community?

    Exercise: Make a list of the most pressing issues in your industry and highlight those that align with your organization's mission.

Step 3: Define the transformative impact you want to achieve

A MTP doesn't just address a problem, it also offers a **clear and meaningful transformation**. You need to define what change you hope to generate.

- Key question: How would people's lives change if your organization achieves its purpose? What concrete improvements will the affected communities experience?

    Exercise: Write a brief description of how your organization will change people's lives. Use active, action-focused verbs: "Improve," "Empower," "Transform," "Create."

Step 4: Scalability: Think Big

Your MTP should be **scalable**, meaning it can grow beyond a local market and have a massive impact. Ask yourself how you can expand the scope of your mission.

- Key question: How can you make your solution replicable globally or in different contexts?

    Exercise: Think about how your model can be applied to different geographies, sectors or audiences. Think about technology platforms or networks that would allow you to expand your impact.

Step 5: Formulate your MTP into a clear statement

Finally, bring all the elements above together to formulate your **MTP into a clear and concise statement**. The language should be simple yet powerful, inspiring and easy to remember.

Exercise: Write a first version of your MTP using this basic format:

- "Our organization seeks [transformative action] for [target group] through [solution], in order to [final impact]."

6.2 Brainstorming templates and tools

Sometimes it can be difficult to bring abstract ideas down to a concrete concept. That's why we've provided you with **brainstorming tools and templates** to help you organize your ideas and create a solid MTP.

Template 1: Impact Map

This map will allow you to visualize the impact of your MTP in different areas of your organization and in people's lives.

1. **Main problem**: What problem are you solving?
2. **Direct Impact**: How will this MTP affect your primary customer?
3. **Secondary impact**: What other sectors or people will be indirectly impacted by your purpose?
4. **Long-term effect**: How will the industry or system change because of your MTP?

Template 2: Scalability matrix

Scalability is key for a MTP. Use this matrix to assess the expansion potential of your purpose.

Ask	Answer	Suggested Action
Can this purpose be replicated in other regions?		
What are the technological or economic barriers to scaling?		
How can you leverage partnerships or networks to amplify impact?		

Template 3: MTP Statement Generator

Complete the following sentences to generate a first version of your MTP:

- **Transformative Action**: We want ___
- **Target Audience**: for [group] who ___
- **Final Impact**: so that they can ___

6.3 Practical examples of MTP in different industries and sectors

Here are some real-world examples of MTP from different industries. These examples will help you understand how organizations across different sectors have used a MTP to create transformative change.

Example 1: Technology
- **Google**: "Organizing the world's information and making it universally accessible and useful."
- **Transformation**: Google revolutionized the way we access information, democratizing knowledge for millions of people.

Example 2: Energy
- **Tesla**: "Accelerating the world's transition to sustainable energy."
- **Transformation**: Tesla has led the electric car revolution, and is driving the use of renewable energy, changing the transportation and energy sectors.

Example 3: Retail and Sustainable Consumption
- **Patagonia**: "We are in business to save our home, the planet."
- **Transformation**: Patagonia has integrated sustainability into all of its business practices, encouraging consumers and other businesses to adopt more environmentally responsible practices.

Example 4: Education
- **Khan Academy**: "Providing a free, world-class education to anyone, anywhere."
- **Transformation**: Online academia has democratized education, offering free access to millions of students around the world.

Example 5: Social Sector
- **Charity: Water**: "Bringing clean, safe drinking water to people in developing countries."
- **Transformation**: Charity: Water has provided millions of people with access to clean water, improving the health and well-being of entire communities.

Conclusion

This chapter has provided you with a practical guide to **creating your own MTP**, with tools, templates, and examples that will allow you to land your purpose in a clear, inspiring, and massive way. Remember that an effective MTP must be scalable, transformative, and have a significant impact on the lives of many people. With these tools, you are on your way to defining a purpose that not only inspires your organization, but also changes the world.

Part II: Implementing and aligning your MTP

Doing something of value, really of value, requires a lot of effort, sacrifice, perseverance, many skills, resources, time and even a little luck. But everything, everything will be worth it, that's for sure.

Reading the great teacher Stephen R. Covey in his book "The 7 Habits of Highly Effective People" taught me something that I don't know why I had missed when years ago I read Albert Einstein profusely and I quote: "Albert Einstein observed that <<the significant problems we face cannot be solved at the same level of thinking we were at when we created them>>.

What does this mean? Well, I would explain it myself, although I prefer to quote the great master:

"When we look around and within ourselves and recognize the problems created as we live and interact with the personality ethic, we begin to understand that these are deep, fundamental problems that cannot be solved at the superficial level in which they were created. We need a new level, a deeper level of thinking – a paradigm based on principles that accurately describe the effectiveness of human beings and their interactions – to overcome these deep concerns."

So what is this all about? Well, **effectiveness**, and there is no one better than the great master, with his apologies I quote him again: "The 7 habits are habits of effectiveness. Because they are based on principles, they provide the maximum possible benefits in the long term. They become the foundations of character, creating a center of empowering correct maps, from which the person can solve problems effectively, maximize their opportunities and continually learn and integrate other principles in an upward spiral of development."

And all this is for? Well, as you know, every company should be effective in every aspect if it wants to survive: sales, innovation, finance, sustainability, human resources, engineering, oh my God! Of course! How should they solve problems? Well, I would say with effectiveness. Developing a Massive Transformative Purpose necessarily implies implementing an effectiveness policy throughout the company. It is such a brutal alignment of the actions and decisions taken in the company with your long-term objectives that even your competition will begin to imitate it.

Chapter 7: How to align your team and organization around MTP?

One of the biggest challenges in creating a **Massive Transformative Purpose (MTP)** is making sure your entire organization is aligned with it. A MTP cannot be successful if it is not embedded in the team's culture, communication, and operations. This chapter is designed to show how you can inspire your team and create an organizational culture where the MTP is the compass that guides all actions and decisions.

7.1 Purposeful leadership: How to inspire your team?

Leadership is critical to aligning your team with the MTP. As a leader, your role is **to inspire, guide, and motivate** your team to not only understand the purpose, but to make it their own. Here are some key elements to leading with purpose:

7.1.1 Be a role model

Leaders must **embody values and purpose** in their daily behavior. This includes making decisions consistent with MTP, treating employees and customers with respect, and demonstrating an unwavering commitment to the impact your organization wants to create.

- **Example**: **Elon Musk** and his focus at Tesla and SpaceX on sustainable energy and space exploration. His purposeful leadership has inspired his teams to work tirelessly towards seemingly unattainable goals.

    Action: Evaluate whether your daily decisions reflect the MTP you have defined. Ask your team how they perceive your leadership in relation to the purpose and adjust based on the feedback received.

7.1.2 Involve everyone in the mission

Involve every team member in defining and executing the MTP. When employees feel **part of the process**, they become more engaged and motivated. It's not just about them understanding the MTP, but about them feeling that they play a key role in achieving it.

- **Example**: Companies like **Zappos** have made their customer service-focused culture the purpose of everyone from management to customer service staff. This has allowed them to offer a unique experience that everyone in the company supports.

Action: Organize brainstorming sessions and regular meetings to discuss how each department or role contributes to the overall mission. Make each employee clear about their impact on MTP.

7.1.3 Constantly reinforce the MTP

A purpose-driven leader consistently reinforces the **MTP message** at every opportunity: in team meetings, emails, and strategic decisions. Keep purpose at the center of the conversation.

- **Example**: **Patagonia**, with its focus on sustainability, reinforces its purpose consistently through its internal and external communication. Leadership encourages employees to adopt sustainable lifestyles that reflect the company's mission.

    Action: During important meetings or updates, always link decisions or progress to the MTP, showing how current accomplishments align with the transformative mission.

7.2 Communication and storytelling tools to generate cohesion

A MTP cannot be effective if it is not **clearly communicated** at all levels of the organization. Storytelling and the right communication tools allow the message to be inspiring, clear and accessible to the entire team.

7.2.1 The power of storytelling in MTP

Storytelling is one of the most powerful tools for communicating purpose. Personal stories and real-life examples allow employees to connect emotionally with the MTP. Telling stories of customers or collaborators who have been impacted by the purpose makes it more tangible.

- **Example**: **TOMS Shoes** uses storytelling to share stories of people who have received shoes through their "buy one, give one" model. This approach has allowed employees and customers to see the direct impact of their purchases, creating a sense of pride and ownership.

    Action: Identify stories within your organization that demonstrate how MTP is changing lives. Make these stories a regular part of your internal communications.

7.2.2 Effective internal communications

Internal communication is essential to ensure that the MTP is understood and shared by everyone. Tools such as newsletters, collaboration platforms, and team meetings allow the purpose to be a constant point of reference.

- **Example**: Companies like **Slack** use their own platform to create communication channels where employees can share news, stories, and discussions related to MTP. This helps keep the mission alive and at the center of daily interactions.

    Action: Establish specific communication channels to share progress related to MTP. Use collaborative platforms where employees can contribute ideas and suggestions to better align work with purpose.

7.2.3 Visualizing the purpose

Using visual elements, such as infographics or posters, helps to **visually remind** employees of the MTP. This reinforces the message without the need to repeat it verbally and allows for a deeper internalization of the purpose.

- **Example**: **Salesforce**, through its purpose of improving communities, uses signage and visuals in its offices to remind employees of its commitment to charitable causes and community projects.

    Action: Create engaging visuals that communicate your MTP and place them in key areas of your office. Also consider sharing infographics on digital channels so that all employees, wherever they are, can see the impact they are making.

7.3 Create a purpose-focused organizational culture

For a MTP to work in the long term, it must be embedded in the **organizational culture**. This means that the MTP values not only guide the company's strategy, but also the way employees collaborate, interact, and make decisions.

7.3.1 Values-based culture

A **values-based organizational culture** is one where everyday decisions are aligned with the transformational purpose. This means that the underlying values of the MTP guide not only strategic actions, but also interpersonal interactions and the development of internal policies.

- **Example**: **Ben & Jerry's** has a culture focused on social justice, which is directly linked to its MTP of creating a positive impact on society. This is reflected in its awareness campaigns and internal initiatives to promote equality.

    Action: Review your company values and ensure they are aligned with MTP. Encourage dialogue about these values and how they should be reflected in daily interactions between employees.

7.3.2 Incentives and recognitions aligned with the MTP

To embed MTP into the organization's culture, it is important that incentives and recognition are also aligned with this purpose. Employees should be rewarded not only for achieving business goals, but also for their contribution to MTP objectives.

- **Example**: Companies like **Unilever** have established sustainability goals within their business model and reward employees who contribute to achieving these goals. This creates an alignment between personal success and the company's overall purpose.

  Action: Define performance indicators that measure not only financial or operational performance, but also the impact each employee has on MTP. Implement a recognition system for those who significantly contribute to the purpose objectives.

7.3.3 Recruiting and developing talent with purpose

An effective MTP not only attracts customers, but also purpose-aligned **talent. Attracting and retaining employees who share the MTP vision is key to a strong and focused organizational culture.**

- **Example**: **Tesla** has been successful in attracting engineers and renewable energy experts who are attracted to its mission of accelerating the transition to sustainability. This attraction of talent allows the company to innovate and execute its MTP effectively.

  Action: Incorporate MTP into your recruiting processes, ensuring that candidates understand and are excited about the organization's mission. Make sure that employees' professional development is also aligned with the transformational mission.

Conclusion

Aligning your team and organization around MTP is essential to its long-term success. Inspiring leadership, effective communication, and a purpose-driven organizational culture are the key pillars to ensure that MTP is understood, embraced, and executed by everyone in the organization.

By following the recommendations in this chapter, you will be able to not only communicate MTP effectively, but also build a culture of purpose where every team member feels that their work has greater meaning and contributes to something transformative.

Chapter 8: Strategies to incorporate MTP into your business model

A **Massive Transformative Purpose (MTP)** can be a fundamental guide to an organization's long-term success, but it is not enough for it to exist in theory or in inspiring words. To truly impact, MTP must be embedded in **daily operations and the business model**. This chapter provides practical strategies for making your MTP an integral part of your organization, from operations to business model design, and discusses cases of companies that have effectively achieved this goal.

8.1 How to integrate MTP into your daily operations

The first step to making your MTP effective is to ensure that it is deeply integrated into your company's daily operations. Every action, decision, and process must align with the purpose you have set.

8.1.1 Align key processes with the MTP

MTP should guide every area of your organization, from supply chain to customer service. Identify critical processes within your organization and assess how they can better align with your purpose.

- **Example**: If your MSP is to improve sustainability in your industry, processes such as raw material procurement or production should be adjusted to minimize environmental impact. This may involve choosing ethical suppliers or adopting circular economy practices.

    Action: Conduct an audit of your key processes and look for opportunities to make adjustments that support your MTP. This may include changes to how you interact with suppliers, how you manage your logistics, or how you measure success in different areas.

8.1.2 Set daily goals related to MTP

It's crucial that your team has **clear, measurable goals** that reflect MTP in daily operations. By defining KPIs (key performance indicators) that are aligned with purpose, you can ensure that impact is consistently measured and achieved.

- **Example**: At a company like **Salesforce**, which has a strong commitment to social equality, HR teams might have specific goals to improve diversity in hiring, while the operations team might focus on sustainability in their supply chain.

    Action: Define specific KPIs that measure the impact of your MTP in key areas such as sustainability, inclusion, or social responsibility, depending on your purpose. These objectives should be reviewed regularly and connected to the organization's overall goals.

8.1.3 Continuing training in the MTP

Ensure employees fully understand how their daily work contributes to MTP. This requires ongoing training, which may include workshops, onboarding sessions, and regular updates on progress toward MTP goals.

- **Example**: **Unilever** trains its employees on how daily decisions in every area of the company can support its mission of sustainability and well-being. This includes training on resource management, waste reduction, and relationships with local communities.

    Action: Design regular training programs that not only include technical skills, but also training on the MTP, its objectives, and how each team member can contribute.

8.2 Sustainable and purposeful business models

A well-executed MTP should influence the design of the **business model**. Companies that truly embed their purpose into their structure focus not only on profitability, but on how purpose can amplify their value in the marketplace, attract customers, and drive innovation.

8.2.1 Design a business model focused on MTP

Your business model should be designed to generate value for both the organization and the community or customers you serve. A purpose-driven business model ensures that social or environmental impact is not just a side effect, but an essential part of success.

- **Example**: **Patagonia** doesn't just sell clothing; their business model is structured to support environmental activism. From donating a portion of their profits to ecological causes to offering free repairs on their products, every aspect of their business is designed to reduce environmental impact.

    Action: Evaluate your current business model and look for ways to incorporate your MTP directly into your product or service offering. Can you add a social or environmental component that will not only enhance your brand image, but also increase the value of what you offer?

8.2.2 Innovation through purpose

Incorporating a MTP into your business model often drives **innovation.** When purpose is at the heart of your strategy, creative solutions and new models naturally emerge to address the challenges and opportunities posed by the MTP.

- **Example: Tesla**, whose MVP is to accelerate the transition to sustainable energy, has developed a range of innovative products including electric vehicles and renewable energy solutions. Its purpose has driven continuous innovation, enhancing its competitive advantage and attracting both customers and investors.

    Action: Foster a culture of MTP-driven innovation within your organization. Create teams dedicated to exploring new ways to achieve purpose and developing innovative products or services that reinforce transformative impact.

8.2.3 Sustainable business models

sustainable business model, both in financial and social and environmental terms. This means that the purpose must generate long-term value without compromising future resources.

- **Example**: Companies like **Beyond Meat** and **Impossible Foods** have created sustainable business models that are not only profitable, but also focus on reducing environmental footprint through plant-based meat production.

    Action: Evaluate the sustainability of your business model and adjust the areas where you can generate more value in the long term, whether through efficient use of resources, waste reduction or commitment to ethical business practices.

8.3 Case studies: Companies that have successfully incorporated their MTP into their strategy

Learning from companies that have successfully integrated their MTP into the core of their business model is key to understanding best practices. Below are some examples of organizations that have achieved success by integrating their purpose holistically.

8.3.1 Tesla: Sustainable energy as a business driver

Purpose: "To accelerate the world's transition to sustainable energy."

Tesla has fully integrated its MTP into its business model, not only making electric cars but also providing renewable energy solutions, such as solar roofs and home batteries. Its purpose has not only driven its product strategy, but also its investments, strategic partnerships, and daily operations.

Key lessons:
- Involve your MTP in every aspect of your product offering.
- Drive innovation as a vehicle to fulfill your purpose.

8.3.2 TOMS: The "Buy One, Give One" Model

Purpose: "To improve people's lives by providing footwear, clean water, and better living conditions."

TOMS pioneered the "buy one, give one" model, where for every pair of shoes sold, the company donated one to a person in need. This MTP not only increased sales, but created a loyal customer base that felt part of something bigger.

Key lessons:
- Engage customers in MTP to build emotional engagement and loyalty.
- Make sure social impact is clearly linked to the value proposition.

8.3.3 Unilever: Sustainability as a growth strategy

Purpose: "To make sustainable development mainstream."

Unilever has integrated sustainability into the heart of its business model, committing to reducing environmental impact and improving the health and wellbeing of the communities in which it operates. Its "Sustainable Living Plan" has enabled its brands to grow faster and become more relevant to consumers.

Key lessons:
- Integrating sustainability can attract conscious consumers and increase competitiveness.
- Having a clear MTP improves the relationship with stakeholders, including employees and investors.

Conclusion

Integrating a **Massive Transformative Purpose** into your business model is crucial to ensure that purpose not only inspires, but also drives growth, innovation, and sustainability. Through aligning operations, building sustainable business models, and learning from real-world examples, your organization can create lasting, transformative impact.

Incorporating a MTP not only changes the way your company operates, but also the way your customers, employees, and investors view you. A well-executed MTP not only drives innovation and growth, but also creates a meaningful legacy that transcends the company itself.

Chapter 9: Resistance to change: How to overcome internal challenges?

One of the main obstacles to implementing a **Massive Transformative Purpose (MTP)** is resistance to change within the organization itself. Although a MTP can offer a clear and compelling vision for the future, many companies face challenges when trying to align their teams and processes with this new direction. This chapter is dedicated to identifying the sources of resistance, managing that pushback, and developing strategies to achieve widespread support across the organization.

9.1 Identify and manage resistance to change

Before you can address resistance to change, it's crucial **to identify its sources**. Resistance can manifest itself in a variety of ways—from skepticism and lack of commitment to outright opposition. Often, this resistance isn't a rejection of the purpose itself, but rather fear of the unknown, discomfort with new roles, or concern about the impact on current work.

9.1.1 Common types of resistance to change

- **Emotional resistance**: People may feel insecure about the possibility of losing control over their work environment or what their future will be like in the organization. This resistance arises from uncertainty and fear of failure.
- **Cognitive resistance**: This occurs when people do not fully understand the **value** of change or see it as unnecessary. Skepticism about whether the MTP is achievable or even relevant can hinder progress.
- **Cultural resistance**: When deeply ingrained values and norms in the organization's culture conflict with the new purpose, it can be difficult to change established habits and mindsets.

9.1.2 Detection of resistance signals

It is important to watch for early signs of resistance, which may include:

- **Delays in implementation**: If MTP-related initiatives are met with constant delays or excuses, it may be an indication of resistance.
- **Decreased productivity**: If teams are showing lower productivity or lack of motivation, it may be because they are not aligned or committed to the new purpose.

- **Low engagement in meetings or training**: Lack of active participation, questions or discussions during meetings may suggest that employees are not internalizing the MTP message.

9.1.3 Resistance management strategies

The key to managing resistance to change is **effective communication** and **empathetic leadership**. It is essential to listen to employees' concerns and respond to them in a way that makes them feel understood and valued.

- **Transparency in communication**: The benefits of MTP and how it will impact the organization need to be clearly explained. Being honest about the challenges and reasons behind the change can allay fears.
- **Empowerment through change**: Involving employees in the MTP implementation process gives them a sense of control and ownership, which reduces resistance.

9.2 Strategies to generate buy-in (support) throughout the organization

A successful MTP requires broad and deep support at all levels of the organization. Gaining that **buy-in** is not just about imposing a purpose, but making it part of the organization's collective identity.

9.2.1 Create a shared vision

The first step to generating buy-in is to create a **shared vision** that resonates with everyone in the organization. The purpose should feel relevant not only to leaders, but also to employees at all levels. To achieve this:

- **Involve everyone from the beginning**: Employees should be part of the MTP formulation process, allowing them to feel that their voice has been heard and that their work is part of something bigger.
- **Alignment with personal values**: MTP should align with employees' values so they feel a personal connection. If you can get employees to see how their work directly contributes to the purpose, they will be more inclined to support it.

9.2.2 Leadership with purpose

Leaders are **role models** for the rest of the organization, so they must demonstrate genuine commitment to MTP. Employees watch the actions of their leaders, and if they perceive inconsistency between talk and action, support can fall apart.

- **Authenticity**: Leaders must communicate MTP passionately and consistently, showing that it is not just a marketing exercise, but a genuine commitment to transformation.
- **Exemplary action**: Leaders must demonstrate through their daily decisions and behaviors how MTP is a priority. This can include strategic decisions, investment commitments, and adjusting the organizational structure to support the purpose.

9.2.3 Training and capacity building around MTP

It is important to provide employees with the **tools necessary** to integrate MTP into their daily work. This can be achieved through training programs and professional development opportunities that align their skills with the needs of the transformative purpose.

- **Tailored Training**: Offer training programs designed for each level of the organization, helping employees understand how their specific role contributes to MTP.
- **Constant communication**: Keep channels open to update employees on MTP progress. This includes regular reports on achievements made, challenges encountered, and how they are being overcome.

9.3 Overcoming cultural and structural barriers

Organizational culture and hierarchical structures can be **powerful barriers** to change. Many companies have a way of doing things that is deeply rooted in their history and traditions. Overcoming these barriers is crucial to the successful implementation of a MTP.

9.3.1 Diagnosis of cultural barriers

A **cultural assessment** is essential to understand how current values and beliefs may hinder the adoption of CTP. The following questions can help identify cultural barriers:

- Are there dominant beliefs or behaviors that conflict with MTP?
- Is today's culture open to change or more conservative and resistant?
- Are there significant differences between the leadership culture and that of the team as a whole?

9.3.2 Cultural readjustment

Once the barriers have been identified, it is necessary **to work on the organizational culture** to align it with the MTP. This does not mean completely eliminating the current culture, but rather adjusting it to be more open to change and transformative purpose.

- **Foster a growth mindset**: Promoting a culture that values innovation, flexibility, and continuous learning is essential to overcoming cultural barriers. Employees should feel safe to experiment and make mistakes without fear of punishment.
- **Celebrate small wins**: Reinforce positive behaviors aligned with MTP through recognition, incentives, and celebrations. This sends a clear message that change is appreciated and rewarded.

9.3.3 Overcoming structural barriers

In many organizations, traditional **hierarchical structures** can slow the adoption of MTP. These structures tend to favor stability over innovation and change, which can hinder the flexibility needed to implement a transformative purpose.

- **Decentralization**: Empowering smaller, autonomous teams within the organization to make decisions quickly around MTP. This allows for greater agility and flexibility.
- **Organizational restructuring**: If necessary, consider restructuring parts of the organization to eliminate silos and facilitate cross-functional collaboration, which is essential to implementing a broad, transformative purpose.

Conclusion

Overcoming resistance to change is one of the biggest challenges when implementing a **Massive Transformative Purpose**. It requires patience, clear and consistent communication, and a strategic approach that takes into account both emotional and structural barriers. This chapter has offered guidance for identifying and managing resistance, building internal support, and overcoming cultural and organizational obstacles. If these challenges are addressed proactively, MTP can become a mobilizing force that will unite the entire organization around a shared vision of transformation.

Part III: Scaling and measuring the impact of your MTP

You have surely heard the phrase: "we must not reinvent the wheel" or "we must not reinvent the wheel", well this is one of those cases, let me explain:

I quote: "There is only one way to get someone to do something. Have you ever stopped to think about it? Yes, only one way. And that is to get the other person to want to do it. Remember, there is no other way… The difference between appreciation and flattery is very simple. One is sincere and the other is not. One comes from the heart; the other comes from the mouth. One is altruistic, the other selfish. One arouses universal admiration; the other is universally condemned." Dale Carnegie.

So, what is the lesson? What is important? First, let us forget about flattery towards others, no matter what, that doesn't work; and then let us honestly and sincerely appreciate the people who deserve it, as a great Peruvian chef said: be generous; although the chef refers to serving a good dish, abundant with food, it applies to our case in question: let us be generous in our displays of approval and praise; that will make us win heaven, in our particular case: May our MTP be successful: accepted, loved, praised by our colleagues and replicated effectively throughout the company.

In this regard, there is a saying that I learned from the great master, for all of us to reflect on, and it goes like this:

"I will pass this way but once; so whatever good I may do, or whatever courtesy I may have for any human being, let it be now. I will not put it off until tomorrow, nor forget it, for I shall never pass this way again."

Rule 2 from the great teacher Dale Carnegie in his book "How to Win Friends and Influence People" is:

"SHOW HONEST AND SINCERE APPRECIATION"

Chapter 10: How to scale your MTP and maximize global impact?

A **Massive Transformative Purpose (MTP)** has the power to change the world, but to do so, it must be scalable. This chapter will explore how to take your MTP to the next level, how to leverage technology tools and exponential platforms to maximize its impact, and how some organizations have already successfully scaled their purpose.

10.1 Tools to scale your purpose

Scalability is critical for a MTP to truly have a massive impact. Once you've defined your purpose and started implementing it, the next challenge is finding ways to replicate and amplify that impact on a global scale. There are multiple approaches and tools to scaling a MTP, ranging from organizational strategies to specific technologies.

10.1.1 Expansion strategies

To scale your MTP, it is crucial to develop an **expansion plan** that allows you to take your purpose to new geographies, markets or sectors. Some key strategies include:

- **Franchising or licensing**: If your purpose has a replicable business model, consider expanding through franchising or licensing, allowing other entrepreneurs to share your purpose while maintaining the integrity of your vision.
- **Strategic Alliances**: Establishing partnerships with other organizations that share similar values and missions can accelerate the expansion of your MTP. These alliances can help you penetrate new markets or access resources that your organization does not have.
- **Organic growth models**: Another strategy is to foster growth within the organization through autonomous teams that can adapt MTP to their local contexts, allowing for more natural and flexible growth.

10.1.2 Repeatability and standardization

One of the key principles for scaling is repeatability. This means that your purpose must be replicable in different places or situations without losing its essence. To achieve this, it is necessary to:

- **Document processes**: Have operational manuals and guides that describe how to implement the MTP, ensuring that all stakeholders understand and execute the purpose consistently.

- **Establish success metrics**: Define key performance indicators (KPIs) that measure the success of your MTP implementation across different environments. These metrics help ensure consistency as you scale.

10.1.3 Ambassador networks

Building a network of **MTP ambassadors** is an effective tool for scaling impact. Ambassadors can be employees, customers, or partners who are deeply committed to your purpose and actively promote it in their communities or professional networks. These individuals can play a crucial role in scaling and maintaining enthusiasm at each stage of growth.

10.2 Using technology and exponential platforms to amplify your MTP

Technology is a key factor in scalability. Organizations that have achieved global impact often use exponential technologies and digital platforms to amplify their efforts. This section will focus on how you can leverage these tools to grow your MTP faster and with fewer resources.

10.2.1 Exponential technologies

Exponential technologies refer to those that experience accelerated growth and have the potential to transform entire industries. These technologies can help you scale your MTP beyond traditional boundaries. Some of the most relevant ones are:

- **Artificial Intelligence (AI)**: AI can help you analyze large volumes of data and generate key insights to optimize your operations, improve decision-making, and customize the impact of your MTP for different audiences.
- **Blockchain**: This technology can bring transparency and security to your operations. If your MTP is related to sustainability or social impact, blockchain can help verify and track the achievements of your purpose, gaining trust among stakeholders.
- **Internet of Things (IoT)**: IoT can collect real-time data on the impact of your initiatives. This is especially useful for organizations that want to accurately measure the environmental or social impact of their actions.

10.2.2 Digital platforms

Digital platforms allow for mass dissemination of a purpose. Thanks to the internet and social media, you can communicate your MTP to a global audience, build communities around your purpose, and foster collaboration between people and organizations from different regions.

- **Social media**: Platforms like Facebook, Instagram, LinkedIn, or Twitter can be powerful tools to amplify your MTP message. Creating engaging content that inspires people to join your purpose can generate viral movements that accelerate scalability.
- **Collaborative platforms**: Tools like Slack, Trello, or Asana can be used to organize global teams working on your MTP implementation, facilitating real-time coordination and collaboration.
- **Crowdsourcing and crowdfunding**: These platforms allow organizations to involve a massive number of people in creating or funding solutions aligned with their MTP. Examples include Kickstarter, GoFundMe, or Change.org, which can help mobilize resources quickly.

10.2.3 Automation as an accelerator of MTP

Automating key processes is an effective strategy for scaling without adding large operational costs. This is especially useful for organizations that want to grow quickly without compromising the quality of their purpose.

- **Marketing Automation**: Using automated marketing platforms (like HubSpot or Mailchimp) can help you effectively spread your MTP to mass audiences without the need for constant human intervention.
- **Operational automation**: In sectors such as manufacturing, logistics or customer service, automation can accelerate the delivery of products or services aligned with your purpose.

10.3 Examples of organizations that have scaled their impact

Learning from organizations that have successfully scaled their transformative purpose can offer valuable insight into how to apply these principles in your own organization. Below are some examples of companies and NGOs that have successfully scaled their MTP.

10.3.1 Tesla: Scalability through technological innovation and global vision

Tesla's MTP is "accelerating the world's transition to sustainable energy." The company has used **exponential technology** in the form of electric vehicles and advanced batteries to fulfill its purpose. Tesla has scaled by leveraging its ability to continuously innovate and by building a global community passionate about its purpose, using platforms like social media and online events to mobilize millions of people.

10.3.2 Patagonia: Scalability with an environmental purpose

Patagonia, the outdoor apparel company, has a MTP focused on sustainability and environmental protection: "We are in business to save our home, planet Earth." Through strategic partnerships and global campaigns, Patagonia has scaled its purpose, promoting a **culture of conscious consumption**. They use digital platforms to educate their customers and mobilize collective efforts to fight climate change.

10.3.3 Wikipedia: Scalability through crowdsourcing

Wikipedia has managed to scale its purpose of "providing free and universal access to knowledge" through a collaborative platform where thousands of people contribute to creating and updating content. Thanks to its open model and the massive participation of volunteers, Wikipedia has achieved a global impact without depending on large financial resources.

10.3.4 Charity:Water: Scalability through crowdfunding platforms

Charity:Water is an NGO dedicated to bringing clean water to communities in developing countries. Their MTP has been scaled globally through **crowdfunding platforms** and viral campaigns that have mobilized millions of people to donate and participate in the cause. They have successfully integrated technology and social media to tell powerful stories, connecting donors with the real impact they are generating.

Conclusion

Scaling a **Massive Transformative Purpose** requires a combination of **strategy**, **technology**, and **community**. In this chapter, we've explored how your organization can scale its impact globally, leveraging exponential tools and platforms, and we've examined inspiring examples of companies and NGOs that have achieved massive change in their respective areas. By implementing these strategies, your MTP can not only transform your organization, but also create lasting and meaningful change in the world.

Chapter 11: Measuring the impact of a MTP: Key indicators

The ability to measure the impact of a **Massive Transformative Purpose (MTP)** is crucial to its success. A well-defined MTP must deliver meaningful and lasting change, and it is essential to have clear tools and metrics to assess its progress and effectiveness. In this chapter, we will explore how to measure the success of a MTP, what key performance indicators (KPIs) are essential, how to measure impact beyond finances, and what tools can help you closely track results.

11.1 How to measure the success of a MTP? Essential KPIs

Measuring the success of a MTP isn't just about assessing financial growth or brand recognition, but about understanding the **real, transformative impact** it's having on people, communities, and the world at large. Essential KPIs should align with the specific purpose and goals of the MTP, and provide a clear, measurable view of how progress is being made toward that massive purpose.

11.1.1 Definition of specific KPIs

An effective KPI is specific, measurable, attainable, relevant and time-bound (SMART). Here are some essential KPIs for a MTP:

- **Social impact KPIs**: These indicators assess how the MTP is influencing people's quality of life. Examples include the number of people benefiting from the purpose, the number of jobs created, or the reduction in social inequalities.
- **Environmental impact KPIs**: These measure how your MTP is contributing to improving the environment. These can include metrics such as carbon emissions reduction, the amount of natural resources preserved, or the level of renewable energy use.
- **Cultural impact KPIs**: These indicators reflect how the MTP is affecting the beliefs, behaviors, or values of a society. An example might be increased public awareness of certain global issues or the adoption of more responsible behaviors (such as recycling or volunteering).
- **Reach KPIs**: These measure the scale of MTP impact, such as the number of countries, regions or communities reached, or the level of engagement in MTP-related campaigns and programs.
- **Engagement KPIs**: These assess the level of support and active participation of employees, customers or partners around the MTP. Indicators such as

employee retention rate, job satisfaction level or social media engagement can be useful.

11.1.2 Define the Baseline

Before implementing a MTP, it is essential to define a **baseline**: the starting point that will allow you to measure the changes brought about by your purpose. To do this, you must collect data that shows the situation before the implementation of the MTP. This data will allow you to make comparisons over time and understand the magnitude of the impact you are achieving.

11.2 Measure the social, environmental and cultural impact, in addition to the financial impact

One of the key principles of an MTP is that it goes beyond traditional financial success. Impact must encompass **social, environmental and cultural dimensions** in addition to economic results. Here's how to measure each of these aspects.

11.2.1 Measuring social impact

Social impact refers to the **positive changes your MTP brings to people and communities**. Some ways to measure it include:

- **Surveys and interviews**: Conduct surveys with your MTP beneficiaries to assess how their quality of life has improved or how their personal or work situation has changed.
- **Case Studies**: Develop detailed studies of people or communities that have been transformed by your purpose.
- **Number of lives impacted**: Calculate how many people have been directly benefited by the actions and programs derived from your MTP.

11.2.2 Measuring environmental impact

Environmental impact measures how your MTP contributes to the **sustainability of the planet**. Some key metrics are:

- **Reducing your carbon footprint**: Measure the tons of CO_2 avoided thanks to your MTP, especially if it is focused on sustainability or environmental conservation.
- **Saving natural resources**: Monitoring the use of water, energy or materials, or the preservation of protected natural areas.
- **Waste and Recycling**: Evaluate how your MTP encourages waste reduction, recycling, and reuse of materials in daily operations.

11.2.3 Measuring cultural impact

Cultural impact can be more intangible, but equally important. It refers to **changes in behaviors, attitudes, and values** of people or societies due to your MTP. Ways to measure it include:

- **Changes in public perception**: Conduct market research or surveys to assess how perceptions of an issue or cause your MTP addresses have changed.
- **Adoption of practices or behaviors**: Measure how many people adopt new practices or values that your MTP promotes, such as sustainability, inclusion, or diversity.
- **Social movements**: Observe the growth of movements or communities around your purpose.

11.2.4 Financial measurement

Although the goal of a MTP is not solely financial, measuring the economic impact is still important, as a financially sustainable organization can scale and sustain its MTP over the long term. Common financial indicators include:

- **Revenue growth**: How has your MTP contributed to revenue growth? This could be due to increased customer loyalty, attracting new markets, or reducing operating costs.
- **Savings generated by sustainable practices**: Implementing strategies aligned with a MTP can reduce costs through energy efficiency, waste reduction or process optimization.
- **Return on Investment (ROI)**: Measuring the ROI of initiatives and campaigns linked to your MTP is crucial to assess the economic viability of continuing to scale your purpose.

11.3 Examples of metrics and tools for monitoring results

Consistent monitoring is essential to know if your MTP is fulfilling its mission. In this section, we will cover some of the most commonly used tools to measure and monitor the impact of a MTP, and examples of key metrics you can implement.

11.3.1 Tools to measure impact

- **Balanced Scorecard**: This tool allows you to measure your organization's performance not only from a financial perspective, but also from the social and environmental impact, customer satisfaction and internal innovation. The Balanced Scorecard makes it easy to monitor KPIs in different areas.

- **B Impact assessment**: Used by companies seeking certification as **B Corporations**, this method measures performance in five key areas: governance, workers, community, environment, and customers. It is ideal for companies with a strong focus on social responsibility.
- **Surveys and questionnaires**: Tools like Google Forms, SurveyMonkey or Typeform can help you collect quantitative and qualitative data from beneficiaries or stakeholders about the impact of your MTP.
- **Impact analysis software**: Platforms such as **Impact Reporting** or **Bright Impact** allow you to manage, analyze and visualize social and environmental impact data in real time. This software automates data collection and analysis, facilitating the continuous measurement of MTP progress.

11.3.2 Examples of key metrics

Below are concrete examples of metrics you can implement depending on your area of impact:

- **Social impact**: Number of people trained, employed or empowered by your MTP. Reduction in poverty rate or improvement in community health.
- **Environmental impact**: Reduction of CO_2 emissions, savings in water or energy consumption, increase in the use of recycled materials.
- **Cultural impact**: Rate of adoption of MTP-aligned behaviors, such as recycling, gender equality, or workplace inclusion.
- **Financial impact**: Increase in sales resulting from campaigns aligned with the MTP, reduction in operating costs or increase in stakeholder investment due to the purpose.

Conclusion

Measuring the impact of a **Massive Transformative Purpose** is a fundamental task to ensure its long-term success. This chapter has broken down the **essential KPIs**, the **different areas of impact** (social, environmental, cultural and financial), and the **tools** available for tracking results. Measuring effectively not only allows you to evaluate the success of your MTP, but also to continually adjust and improve it to maximize its overall impact.

Chapter 12: Financing and sustainability of the MTP

A **Massive Transformative Purpose (MTP)** requires not only a clear vision and deep commitment, but also solid financing and sustainability strategies that ensure its continuity and expansion in the long term. This chapter focuses on how to finance your MTP effectively, explore different sources of financing, and learn from success stories that have achieved purpose-centered financial models.

12.1 How to finance your long-term purpose

Financing a long-term MTP involves developing strategies that ensure economic sustainability without compromising values and social or environmental impact. Below are the main ways to finance your MTP:

12.1.1 Integrate financial sustainability into business strategy

To ensure your MTP is financially sustainable, it is essential that sustainability is integrated into your business strategy from the start.

- **Inclusive business models**: Design a business model that generates enough revenue to fund MTP initiatives. This can include selling purpose-aligned products or services, subscriptions, licensing, etc.
  Example : **Patagonia** not only sells outdoor apparel, but also offers free repair services to extend the life of their products, fostering sustainability and reducing costs in the long run.
- **Revenue diversification**: Don't rely solely on one revenue stream. Diversifying your revenue streams can help stabilize finances and ensure that MTP initiatives continue even if one source fails.
  Example: **Unilever** has diversified its revenue by creating multiple brands that address different aspects of sustainability and social good, thereby reducing financial risk.

12.1.2 Long-term financial planning

Financial planning is crucial to the sustainability of the CFP. This includes:

- **Strategic budgeting**: Allocate specific resources to initiatives aligned with the MTP. Ensure that there is a dedicated budget to fund long-term projects without relying solely on fluctuating revenues.
- **Financial projections**: Develop financial projections that incorporate the costs and benefits associated with the MFP. This will help you anticipate future funding needs and plan accordingly.

- **Risk management**: Identify and mitigate financial risks that may affect the sustainability of the MTP. This may include creating emergency reserves, insurance or contingency plans.

12.1.3 Reinvest in the MTP

Reinvesting profits in the MTP is an effective strategy to ensure its growth and sustainability.

- **Profit Reinvestment**: Allocate a percentage of net profits to initiatives that amplify the impact of MTP. This can include geographic expansion, new product development, or operational improvements. **Example**: **Tesla** reinvests a significant portion of its revenue into research and development to advance sustainable technologies like batteries and solar energy.
- **Reserve Funds**: Create reserve funds specifically designated to finance future MTP projects. These funds can help cover unforeseen costs or take advantage of growth opportunities.

12.2 Impact investments, crowdfunding and other sources

There are a variety of funding sources that can support a MTP. Some of the most effective ones are explored below:

12.2.1 Impact investments

Impact investments seek to generate financial returns alongside a positive social or environmental impact. This type of investment is ideal for organizations with a clear MTP that want to attract investors committed to social change.

- **Types of impact investments**:
  - **Social venture capital**: Investors looking for startups with high potential for social impact.
  - **Social Impact Bonds**: Financial instruments intended to finance projects with specific social objectives.
  - **Impact funds**: Funds that invest in multiple projects aligned with a social or environmental purpose.
- **Advantages**:
  - Access to significant capital without giving up control of the organization.
  - Strategic support and networking provided by investors.

- **Example**: **Triodos Bank** is a bank that specializes in impact investments, financing projects that promote environmental sustainability and social development.

12.2.2 Crowdfunding

Crowdfunding is an effective way of raising funds through small contributions from a large number of people, usually through online platforms.

- **Popular platforms**:
    - **Kickstarter**: Ideal for creative and technological projects.
    - **Indiegogo**: Flexible, suitable for a variety of projects.
    - **GoFundMe**: Focused on personal and social causes.
    - **Crowdcube**: For funding startups in exchange for equity participation.
- **Strategies for success in crowdfunding**:
    - **Compelling narrative**: Tell an emotional story that connects with potential donors.
    - **Attractive rewards**: Offer incentives to contributors, such as exclusive products or recognition.
    - **Active promotion**: Use social media, email marketing and other channels to spread the word about your campaign.
- **Example**: **Pebble Technology** raised millions through Kickstarter to launch its smartwatch, demonstrating how a well-executed crowdfunding campaign can fund innovative projects.

12.2.3 Grants and public funds

Grants and **public funds** are sources of financing that do not require repayment or equity participation.

- **Sources of grants**:
    - **Governments**: Government programs that support social and environmental initiatives.
    - **Foundations**: Philanthropic organizations that provide funding to projects aligned with their missions.
    - **International institutions**: Organizations such as the United Nations or the World Bank that finance sustainable development projects.

- **Advantages**:
    - It does not dilute the ownership of the company.
    - Provides significant funding for specific projects.
- **Example**: **Charity:Water** has received grants from various international foundations to fund its projects to provide access to clean water in developing countries.

12.2.4 Acceleration programs and incubators

Acceleration programs and incubators offer not only funding, but also mentoring, resources and access to networks.

- **Benefits**:
    - Strategic support and training.
    - Access to a network of potential investors and partners.
    - Operational and technological resources.
- **Example**: **Techstars** offers acceleration programs that include seed investment, mentoring, and access to a global community of entrepreneurs and investors.

12.2.5 Strategic alliances and corporate sponsorships

Forming **strategic alliances** with other organizations or seeking **corporate sponsorships** can provide additional resources and increase the reach of the MTP.

- **Advantages**:
    - Access to financial and non-financial resources.
    - Greater visibility and credibility.
    - Collaboration on joint initiatives that amplify impact.
- **Example**: **Starbucks** has formed partnerships with environmental organizations to promote sustainable practices in its supply chain, reinforcing its commitment to sustainability MTP.

12.3 Success stories of purpose-focused financial models

Analyzing success stories can provide valuable insight into how other organizations have managed to fund and sustain their MTP. Below are three standout examples:

12.3.1 Patagonia: Financial sustainability through the integration of the MTP

Purpose: "We are in business to save our home, planet Earth."

Patagonia has achieved exceptional **financial sustainability** by integrating its sustainability MTP into every aspect of its business model. Some of the key strategies include:

- **Circular business model:** They offer product repair and reuse services, reducing waste and fostering customer loyalty.
- **Purposeful marketing:** Their advertising campaigns emphasize sustainability and environmental responsibility, attracting conscious consumers.
- **Investments in renewable energy:** They have invested in clean energy projects to reduce their carbon footprint and support their sustainability purpose.

Results:

- **Sustained growth:** Patagonia has experienced consistent growth, proving that sustainability can be profitable.
- **Customer Loyalty:** Their focus on sustainability has created a loyal customer base who value and support their purpose.

12.3.2 Ben & Jerry's: Financing through social responsibility

Purpose: "To make the best possible product, respecting people and the planet."

Ben & Jerry's has successfully funded and sustained its MTP through a combination of innovative financial strategies and an unwavering commitment to its social and environmental values.

- **Dual business model:** In addition to selling high-quality ice cream, Ben & Jerry's integrates its purpose into all of its operations, from ethical ingredient sourcing to fair and sustainable labor practices.
- **Social investments:** Part of their profits are allocated to social and environmental initiatives, such as fair trade programs and environmental sustainability projects.
- **Purpose-driven marketing:** Their advertising and public relations campaigns highlight their commitment to social causes, attracting consumers who share their values.

Results:

- **Brand Recognition:** Ben & Jerry's is widely recognized not only for its products, but also for its social and environmental commitment, which strengthens its customer loyalty.

- **Financial Growth:** Despite its focus on purpose, Ben & Jerry's has maintained consistent financial growth, proving that a focus on values can coexist with profitability.

12.3.3 Beyond Meat: Financial innovation and environmental purpose

Purpose: "To create plant-based products that are better for animals, the environment, human health and the climate."

Beyond Meat has managed to scale its MTP by combining **technological innovation**, **strategic financing**, and **commercial alliances**.

- **Product Innovation:** They have developed innovative products that replicate the texture and flavor of animal meat, appealing to both vegan and non-vegan consumers.
- **Investments and Funding:** Beyond Meat has secured significant venture capital investments and gone public, providing them with the resources to expand rapidly.
- **Commercial Alliances:** They have formed alliances with large restaurant and supermarket chains, expanding their reach and availability globally.

Results:

- **Rapid expansion:** Beyond Meat has managed to expand rapidly into international markets, increasing its environmental impact by reducing its dependence on animal meat.
- **Recognition and adoption:** Their focus on innovation and purpose has led to high adoption of their products, establishing themselves as leaders in the plant-based food industry.

Conclusion

Funding and sustaining a **Massive Transformative Purpose** is a challenge that requires strategic planning, a deep understanding of different funding sources, and an ongoing commitment to financial sustainability. This chapter has explored various strategies to fund your MTP over the long term, including impact investing, crowdfunding, grants, and strategic partnerships. In addition, we have analyzed success stories that demonstrate how leading organizations have managed to integrate their purpose into their financial models, ensuring both transformative impact and profitability.

By applying these strategies and learning from these examples, your organization will be better equipped to fund and sustain your MTP, ensuring that purpose not only inspires, but also has the capacity to transform the world in lasting and meaningful ways.

This chapter has provided you with a comprehensive guide on how to fund and ensure the sustainability of your **Massive Transformative Purpose.** From integrating financial sustainability into your business strategy to exploring various funding sources and learning from success stories, you now have the tools to ensure your MTP is not only an inspiring vision, but also a financially viable and sustainable reality in the long term.

In the next chapter, we'll dive into how to **effectively communicate your MTP,** ensuring your message comes across clearly and compellingly to all key stakeholders, including employees, customers and investors.

Part IV: Inspiration and community

Have you ever wondered what kind of leaders we need? Or even better: How many of the leaders we currently have are capable? I can help a little with this point: In a postgraduate course I took at MIT, I was given a shocking fact, and I quote:

"Only 11% of organizations reported having an "established" or "very established" leadership bench (this is the lowest percentage reported in the past 10 years)..." Source: Forbes, 2021.

11% Ladies and gentlemen, so what are we up against? The challenge is really great, we must first be aware of the reality: the problem exists and it is enormous, we must face it, recognize it, study it and then attack it, solve it, part by part, step by step with courage and resilience. One of the ways is to create good leaders, lay the foundations for good leadership, leadership with purpose, effective, responsible and humane.

So I asked myself the following question:

What qualities does a good leader/businessman need to have to carry out a MTP?

First, I repeat, because it is important to be very clear: Creating a **Massive Transformative Purpose (MTP)** is not simply a business decision, it is a call to generate a positive and lasting impact on the world. For an entrepreneur to reach that point of deep inspiration and make the decision to develop a MTP, there must be a series of influences and motivations that guide him on that path. These sources of inspiration are usually personal, professional and contextual, and they can make the difference between a company that only seeks profits and one that aspires to change the world.

Here I detail the main sources of inspiration that I think usually motivate leaders / entrepreneurs to create a MTP:

1. Personal passion for positive change

One of the most powerful sources of inspiration for an entrepreneur is **personal passion**. Many business leaders who create a MTP do so because they have a **genuine and deep interest in solving a social, environmental or human problem**. This passion can be born from personal experiences, frustrations with injustices or a clear perception that the world needs a transformation in some specific area.

For example, Elon Musk created Tesla with the vision of reducing dependence on fossil fuels and mitigating climate change, a concern that was born out of his personal interest in the environment and sustainability.

Key Question: What issue touches you deeply? What injustice, problem or need so outrages you that you feel compelled to act?

2. Direct experience with a social or environmental problem

Another source of inspiration can come from having experienced or witnessed a social or environmental problem firsthand. Sometimes, entrepreneurs are faced with realities they cannot ignore, and this awakens a strong desire to act.

For example, an entrepreneur who grew up in a community with limited access to clean water may be inspired to create a business whose MTP is to provide clean water to rural areas. Having experienced a lack of resources, he has an emotional and practical connection to the problem, which motivates him to use his business platform to make a difference.

Key question: What social or environmental problems have you experienced firsthand that could motivate you to use your company as a driving force for change?

3. Role models and inspiring examples

Examples of **other entrepreneurs who have achieved great things with a MTP** can also be a key source of inspiration. Seeing how other leaders have used their businesses to create a positive impact on the world can show you that it is possible and that you, too, can follow that path.

Stories like that of **Yvon Chouinard**, founder of Patagonia, who has turned his company into an emblem of environmental activism, or that of **Muhammad Yunus**, who founded Grameen Bank to combat poverty through microcredit, can inspire you to think big and use your company as a vehicle for good.

Key Question: Do you know any business leaders who have created a positive impact and whose actions inspire you to do the same?

4. Demands of consumers and new generations

Today, consumers, especially younger ones, are more interested than ever in supporting companies that have an authentic purpose and contribute to the well-being of the planet and society. This conscious consumer trend can be a powerful source of inspiration for an entrepreneur who wants to better connect with their audience and differentiate themselves in a competitive market.

The fact that **younger generations** are demanding more social and environmental responsibility from companies can push leaders to rethink their vision and create a MTP that is aligned with their customers' expectations. This not only ensures a positive impact, but also reinforces customer loyalty.

Key question: What are today's customers looking for in companies? How can you offer them something beyond a product or service?

5. Social and moral responsibility

For many entrepreneurs, the idea of creating a MTP stems from a **sense of responsibility** to the world. They know that with their economic power and influence, they have a **unique opportunity to do good** and give back to society. This sense of moral responsibility can be a powerful inspiration for those looking to give greater meaning to their work.

Entrepreneurs who feel that their success should not only be measured in financial terms, but also by the positive impact they generate, are aligned with the idea of a MTP. This approach also helps to balance traditional capitalism with a more conscious and responsible approach.

Key Question: Do you feel a responsibility to society and the world that inspires you to use your business to create positive change?

6. A long-term vision of the future of the world

Some entrepreneurs are inspired by their vision of the future. As they look at where the world is headed, whether in terms of technology, sustainability or human well-being, they realize that their company can be part of that future. **Visualizing a better world** and seeing how your business can play a part in that process can be a key source of motivation.

This long-term vision, combined with the desire to leave a positive legacy, leads entrepreneurs to think big and create a MTP that is aligned with the direction in which the world must move to improve.

Key question: How do you envision the future and what role do you think your company can play in creating that future?

7. Connection with the community and the environment

Many entrepreneurs find inspiration in their **local communities** or the places where they live and operate. They want to give back to the community that has supported them, improve the living conditions of the people around them, or protect the natural resources they depend on.

The connection with the local community, whether in social, economic or environmental terms, can awaken in the entrepreneur a strong desire to **preserve or improve their environment**, which in turn leads to the creation of a MTP. This type of local inspiration can have a global impact if amplified correctly.

Key question: What aspects of your community or environment would you like to protect or improve through your company?

8. The search for a lasting legacy

Finally, one of the greatest sources of inspiration for an entrepreneur when creating a MTP is the **quest for a lasting legacy**. Most successful entrepreneurs eventually ask themselves: **What will remain after me? How do I want to be remembered?**

A MTP offers the opportunity to create a legacy that goes beyond financial success or business achievements. It allows the entrepreneur to be remembered for having changed lives, solved global problems or contributed to the well-being of the planet.

Key question: What kind of legacy would you like to leave through your company and how can a MTP help you achieve it?

Reflection: The inspiration to create a MTP

Creating a MTP doesn't just require an idea or a strategy; it requires **deep inspiration** and a connection to what really matters to you and your environment. Whether it comes from personal experiences, a passion for solving a problem, the influence of other leaders, or responsibility to society, the key is to **find what moves you** to make a change.

A MTP is a bold, transformative statement that has the potential to leave a positive mark on the world. The source of inspiration for an entrepreneur looking to embark on this journey can come from many directions, but most importantly, it must come from a genuine and authentic place.

Chapter 13: Inspiring stories of leaders with MTP

Massive Transformative Purpose (MTP) has been adopted by many visionary leaders around the world, who have succeeded in inspiring, mobilizing and transforming their organizations and communities. This chapter will focus on success stories, where leaders have implemented MTP in their projects, companies or initiatives, generating deep and scalable changes. In addition, we will analyze the key lessons that you can apply to shape your own MTP.

13.1 Interviews or inspiring stories from leaders who have implemented a MTP

This section compiles examples of leaders who have implemented a MTP, showing how their visions not only transformed their organizations, but also created significant social impact. Here are some inspiring stories:

13.1.1 Elon Musk - Tesla and SpaceX: Accelerating the transition to sustainable energy and space exploration

Elon Musk's MTP through **Tesla** and **SpaceX** has redefined entire industries. Tesla aims to "accelerate the world's transition to sustainable energy." This vision has not only revolutionized the automotive industry, but has also driven innovation in batteries and solar energy. In the case of SpaceX, their purpose is to "make humanity a multi-planetary species," which has led to unprecedented advancements in space exploration.

Key lesson: Musk's ambition to transform industrial sectors is based on a clear and bold purpose, which has the potential to improve both life on Earth and the survival of humanity. The key is to think big and tackle global problems.

13.1.2 Yvon Chouinard - Patagonia: Saving the planet

Patagonia, the outdoor apparel company founded by **Yvon Chouinard**, has a MTP focused on preserving the environment: "We are in business to save our home, planet Earth." Chouinard has adopted sustainable business practices, donating 1% of sales to environmental causes, and recently transferred ownership of the company to ensure all profits are reinvested into protecting the planet.

Key Lesson: Authenticity and commitment to a long-term purpose can redefine how a company operates. Patagonia is not only profitable, but has inspired other companies to adopt more sustainable and purpose-driven business models.

13.1.3 Muhammad Yunus - Grameen Bank: Eradicating poverty through microcredits

Muhammad Yunus, founder of the **Grameen Bank**, established a microfinance institution to "eradicate global poverty" through microcredit. By offering small, unsecured loans to low-income people, primarily women, Yunus helped lift millions out of poverty, earning him the Nobel Peace Prize for his contribution.

Key Lesson: Sometimes a simple solution can transform lives. Identifying a fundamental problem and developing an accessible, replicable solution can create significant social change.

13.1.4 Sheryl Sandberg - Lean In: Empowering women in the workplace

Sheryl Sandberg, Facebook's COO and author of "Lean In," launched a global movement to empower women in the workplace. Her MTP is "achieving gender equality at work," and she has inspired millions of women to advance their careers and overcome social and structural barriers.

Key Lesson: A MTP can emerge from an urgent social cause. Sandberg identified a specific problem (gender inequality) and created a movement that is accessible and applicable in multiple settings, from corporations to NGOs.

13.1.5 Marc Benioff - Salesforce: A business as a platform for social change

Marc Benioff, CEO of **Salesforce**, developed a MTP that combines business success with social responsibility. Salesforce has committed to being a carbon neutral company and has implemented a 1% donation model (of its time, products, and resources) to social causes. Benioff is also an advocate for equal pay and social justice.

Key Lesson: A MTP can go beyond a company's core product, encompassing how it operates internally and how it gives back to society. Incorporating ethical and sustainable principles into all aspects of business can elevate both an organization's impact and reputation.

13.2 Key lessons you can apply to your own transformative purpose

The stories of these leaders are pure inspiration for any entrepreneur, leader, or founder looking to implement a MTP. From their experiences, we can draw valuable lessons that will help you create and hone your own transformative purpose.

13.2.1 Think big, but start small

Leaders who have implemented successful MTP didn't start by solving every problem right away. They started by focusing on one specific aspect and scaled it up. Whether addressing an environmental, social, or economic problem, it's important to have a bold vision, but start with tangible, achievable steps.

- **Example**: Muhammad Yunus started with small microcredits in a village in Bangladesh before scaling his initiative globally.

13.2.2 Authenticity as a fundamental pillar

A MTP must be genuine. If it is seen as just a marketing strategy, it will quickly lose credibility. Leaders like Patagonia's Yvon Chouinard don't just talk about sustainability, they live and breathe their values in every aspect of their company.

- **Tip**: Make sure your MTP is aligned with your personal values and those of your organization. Authenticity builds trust and loyal followers.

13.2.3 Collaboration is key

No MTP achieves large-scale impact without collaboration. Whether through strategic partnerships, movement building, or community mobilization, successful leaders are those who understand that they can't do it all alone.

- **Example**: Salesforce, under the leadership of Marc Benioff, has worked closely with NGOs, governments, and other companies to advance social and environmental causes.

13.2.4 Continuous innovation as a driving force of MTP

A MTP is not static. It must evolve and adapt as the world's needs change. Leaders like Elon Musk continue to innovate, not only in their products, but also in their methods of achieving their goals.

- **Tip**: Always look for ways to improve and expand the reach of your MTP. Innovation can open up new opportunities and solutions that were not previously visible.

13.2.5 Long-term impact matters more than short-term recognition

Patience and persistence are essential when it comes to MTP. Some results may take years or decades to materialize, but the most successful leaders are those who are committed to their long-term purpose.

- **Example**: SpaceX's Mars MTP is a long-term project that requires decades of technological development and advancement, but the potential impact is immense.

Conclusion

The stories of leaders like Elon Musk, Yvon Chouinard, Muhammad Yunus, Sheryl Sandberg, and Marc Benioff are beacons of inspiration for anyone looking to implement a MTP. These individuals have not only transformed their industries and organizations, but have also created profound social, economic, and environmental change.

By applying key lessons from their successes—think big, act authentically, collaborate, innovate, and have patience—you can develop your own MTP and scale to create a meaningful impact in the world.

Chapter 14: Building a global community around your MTP

Massive Transformative Purpose (MTP) has powerful potential to create change, not just within your organization, but globally. However, a MTP cannot be done alone; it needs an engaged community to support it and drive it forward. This chapter will explore how you can build and nurture a global community around your purpose, engaging allies, supporters and consumers to maximize the impact of your MTP.

14.1 How to create a supportive community around your purpose

For a MTP to be successful, it is vital that you build a community that shares and supports your vision. These people will not only support your mission, but will also help amplify your message and create a broader impact.

14.1.1 Define your audience

The first step in building a community is to identify the people or groups who share your MTP's core values. Who will benefit from the impact of your purpose? What types of people or entities will be willing to support and promote it?

- **Segmenting your audience**: You can start by identifying key groups, such as employees, customers, strategic partners, NGOs or governments, that have common interests.

14.1.2 Clear and consistent communication

Once you have identified your audience, you need to communicate your MTP clearly and effectively. An inspiring message that reflects authenticity and commitment will help attract more people to your community.

- **Communication Tools**: Use multiple communication channels, such as social media, blogs, newsletters, and events, to share updates, stories, and achievements that demonstrate how your MTP is making an impact.

14.1.3 Create spaces for collaboration

Building a community requires spaces where people can interact and share ideas around your purpose. This not only strengthens the bonds between community members, but also provides opportunities to co-create solutions.

- **Engagement platforms**: You can create groups on social networks, online forums or even organize events where members of your community can actively participate in discussions and projects related to your MTP.

14.1.4 Promote active participation

Actively involve your community in decisions and projects related to your MTP. By offering opportunities for people to participate, whether as volunteers, ambassadors or collaborators, you create a sense of ownership and commitment.

- **Recognition**: Make sure to recognize the achievements of your community members, highlighting the impact they are making by contributing to your purpose.

14.2 Strategies to involve allies, collaborators and consumers

A successful community is not limited to your direct customers or followers. You must attract strategic allies, collaborators and consumers who amplify your message and help take your MTP to new horizons.

14.2.1 Establish strategic collaborations

For a MTP to have a massive impact, it is important to collaborate with organizations, individuals or institutions that share your values and goals. Strategic alliances can increase credibility and the resources available to achieve your mission.

- **Identifying allies**: Look for NGOs, companies, universities or governments that are aligned with your purpose and that can benefit from partnering with you.
- **Mutual benefit**: Make sure that collaborations create value for both parties. Partnerships should be based on a relationship of trust and the pursuit of common goals.

14.2.2 Engaging consumers as MTP ambassadors

Today's consumers aren't just looking for products or services, they also want to support brands and organizations that reflect their values. By aligning your purpose with your consumers' needs and desires, you can turn them into ambassadors for your MTP.

- **Personal Stories**: Invite your customers to share how MTP has impacted them personally or how they believe your organization is making a difference. This humanizes your brand and creates an emotional bond with your community.
- **Rewards and recognition**: Offer incentives for consumers to participate in your MTP promotional campaigns, from symbolic rewards to exclusive discounts.

14.2.3 Collective Mobilization

One of the most effective ways to create impact on a large scale is to mobilize your community around causes related to your MTP. This can take the form of global campaigns, volunteer projects, or specific actions to address a social or environmental issue.

- **Social or Environmental Campaigns**: Design campaigns that resonate with your community's values, inviting participants to contribute their time, talent or resources.
- **Support common causes**: In addition to your own initiatives, show support for other organizations or movements that share your goals by collaborating on joint events, campaigns and projects.

14.3 The Power of Global Movements and Collective Impact

A MTP has the potential to grow beyond the boundaries of your organization, becoming a global movement that inspires and connects people around the world. Here we will explore how to harness the power of movements and collective impact.

14.3.1 The creation of a movement

Global movements are built around ideas and values that transcend geographic, cultural, and economic boundaries. When you get your MTP to resonate with people from different backgrounds, it begins to come to life as a movement.

- **Shared vision**: A movement is fueled by a vision shared by millions of people. It is important that the MTP is articulated in a way that is understandable and relevant to different audiences globally.
- **Collective action**: Movements are strengthened through action. Whether through social activism, volunteering, or simple purchasing decisions, people who are part of the movement must feel that their individual actions contribute to collective change.

14.3.2 Harnessing the power of technology

In an interconnected world, technology is an essential vehicle for scaling a MTP into a global movement. Digital platforms such as social media, apps and websites offer tools to connect like-minded people, no matter where they are.

- **Community Platforms**: Create platforms where your community can interact, share stories, organize, and mobilize for your purpose. These platforms should be accessible and easy to use.

- **Viral content**: Use the power of social media to spread your MTP through inspiring and educational content that can be shared widely. Videos, infographics, and viral campaigns are effective tools to reach millions of people.

14.3.3 Collective Impact

The impact of a MTP comes not just from individual actions, but from the cumulative power of a global community. As more people join the movement, its strength grows exponentially, generating deeper and longer-lasting change.

- **Measuring impact**: Measure the collective impact of your community to demonstrate how working together is contributing to tangible change. Sharing these metrics motivates participants to continue to engage.
- **Global scalability**: As your community grows, it is essential that your actions and goals scale as well. Design projects and campaigns that can be replicated in different contexts and regions, maximizing the reach of your MTP.

Conclusion

Building a global community around your **Massive Transformative Purpose** is an essential process to scaling your impact and achieving large-scale transformation. By identifying and connecting with allies, collaborators, consumers, and activists who share your values, you can create a movement that transcends the boundaries of your organization.

This chapter has provided you with strategies and tools to engage people from different backgrounds and cultures, and to harness the power of global movements and collective impact. A MTP is strongest when it is shared, championed and promoted by an engaged community.

Chapter 15: The future of MTP: How to evolve with your purpose?

Massive Transformative Purpose (MTP) is not static. To stay relevant and continue to generate meaningful impact, you must adapt to the world's changing circumstances and take advantage of new opportunities. This final chapter addresses how your MTP can evolve over time, how to anticipate future trends, and the importance of resilience to sustain your mission in the long term.

15.1 Adaptability and evolution of MTP in a constantly changing world

We live in a rapidly changing environment driven by technology, globalization, climate change and societal evolution. In this context, it is essential that the MTP remains flexible and evolves to remain relevant.

15.1.1 Keep a clear, but flexible vision

The MTP must be robust enough to not lose its essence, but also flexible enough to adapt to new realities. The key is to keep your core purpose intact, while adjusting strategies to implement it.

- **Example: Patagonia** 's purpose of saving the planet has remained the same, but the company has adapted its products and business practices in response to new environmental discoveries and evolving market needs.

15.1.2 Review and evaluate the MTP periodically

Regularly reviewing the impact and relevance of your MTP is essential. As economic, social or technological conditions change, it is necessary to re-evaluate whether the actions you are taking are still the most effective in achieving your purpose.

- **Tip**: Create spaces to reflect on your MTP progress with your team and seek external feedback from stakeholders. This constant evaluation will allow you to detect areas that require adjustment.

15.1.3 Responding to new demands and expectations

Customer, employee and stakeholder expectations are constantly changing. Today, younger generations are demanding more transparency, sustainability and social responsibility from companies. MTP must respond to these new demands to continue to attract support and relevance.

- **Example: Microsoft** has aligned its MTP with a strong focus on sustainability and social good, investing in renewable energy and community programs.

15.2 Anticipation of trends and new opportunities for the purpose

The future world presents challenges, but also opportunities. As new technologies develop and social movements emerge, organizations must anticipate and adapt to these trends to maximize the impact of their MTP.

15.2.1 Exponential technologies and their impact on MTP

Rapid technological evolution can be a key driver for the expansion of a MTP. Tools such as artificial intelligence, blockchain and biotechnology can amplify the scope of purposes, enable greater efficiency in the execution of strategies and improve the measurement of impact.

- **Example**: **SpaceX** has used technological advances in reusable rockets to reduce the costs of space travel, aligning with its MTP of making humanity multi-planetary.

15.2.2 Anticipate social and environmental changes

Climate change, equality movements and demographic shifts create new areas where MTPs can influence. Anticipating and aligning with these changes allows your organisation to be a pioneer and respond to emerging societal needs.

- **Tip**: Keep a long-term view and analyze how new social or environmental realities can impact your purpose. Organizations that anticipate these trends can adapt their MTPs to remain agents of change.

15.2.3 Taking advantage of new market opportunities

Opportunities are constantly emerging in global and digital markets. New business areas, such as renewable energy, circular economy, or digital wellbeing, can be aligned with your MTP to create even more impact and generate new revenue streams.

- **Example**: **Tesla**, seeing an opportunity in the energy industry, expanded its purpose beyond electric cars and launched solar energy solutions, aligning with its sustainability MTP.

15.3 The importance of resilience in the long-term mission

An ambitious MTP is not without its challenges. Staying true to your purpose over the years requires a great deal of resilience and adaptability.

15.3.1 Overcoming challenges and resistance

When implementing a transformative MTP, you are likely to face internal and external resistance, from bureaucratic obstacles to changes in the economy or technology. Resilience is the ability to overcome these challenges without losing sight of the original purpose.

- **Example**: **Elon Musk** faced numerous financial and technical obstacles in developing SpaceX and Tesla, but his resilience and commitment to his transformative purpose allowed him to weather crises and eventual success.

15.3.2 Establish a resilient organizational culture

An organization that embraces change and fosters a culture of adaptability can better withstand crises. Resilience comes not only from leadership, but from every team member, who must be aligned with the MTP and prepared to face challenges.

- **Tip**: Foster a culture of continuous learning and adaptability. A team that is aligned and committed to the purpose will be able to overcome obstacles and find innovative solutions to problems.

15.3.3 Perseverance and commitment to the long-term purpose

A MTP doesn't always produce immediate results. Resilience is also about maintaining perseverance over time, even when the benefits aren't immediately apparent. Long-term commitment to a purpose can make all the difference in your ultimate success.

- **Example**: Muhammad Yunus's mission to eradicate global poverty through microcredit took decades to show its impact on a large scale, but his persistence proved instrumental in achieving meaningful change.

Conclusion

The future of MTP is full of opportunities and challenges. As the world changes rapidly, leaders and organizations that manage to maintain flexibility, anticipate new trends, and cultivate resilience will be the ones that stay ahead of the global impact.

This chapter highlights that a MTP is not a fixed destination, but rather an ongoing journey that must adapt and evolve to maximize its impact. As circumstances change, so must your purpose, to ensure it remains relevant and transformative for future generations.

Maintaining a clear but flexible vision, anticipating trends and being resilient in times of crisis are the keys to your MTP not only surviving, but thriving in the world of tomorrow.

Conclusion, Final Reflection and Summary

N°1. Final conclusion of the key steps to create and implement a MTP

Dear reader, entrepreneur, colleague and leader, I hope with all my strength and with the best of good vibes that this has been at least an eye-opening journey and if it was inspiring, even better. **The world needs you**, it needs entrepreneurs, strong and determined leaders, with purpose, serious, who see the future with optimism and take action to make a better tomorrow.

It is very important to be very clear that creating and implementing a **Massive Transformative Purpose (MTP)** is not just an inspiring exercise, but a key strategy to transform an organization, attract talent and generate a profound impact on society. Below is a summary of the most important steps to create an effective MTP and ensure that it is an integral part of your organization:

1. Discover your core purpose

The first step in developing a MTP is **to identify your organization's core purpose**. This involves a deep introspection on your current values, mission, and vision. Ask yourself:

- What do we want to achieve as an organization beyond economic profit?
- How can we positively change the world?

For this process, follow these key steps:

- **Reflect on your mission and vision**: How do they align with the positive change you want to generate?
- **Identify your core values**: These will be the anchor of your MTP.
- **Define what impact you want to have**: Your MTP should be connected to a cause that has a significant effect on a large scale.

2. Criteria for creating a truly transformative MTP

A MTP should not only be inspiring, but also ambitious and achievable. It should be scalable and clear enough to make an impact. Make sure your MTP meets these essential criteria:

- **Scalability**: The purpose should be broad enough to impact a large number of people. Ask yourself: How can this purpose grow globally?

- **Transformational**: A MTP should be transformational. Think about how it can change people's lives or solve a pressing problem.
- **Clarity and specificity**: Language is crucial. Define your MTP clearly and specifically so that it inspires others to join in.

3. Create the MTP with your team

To ensure your MTP is successful, **align your team** with the purpose and make sure everyone in the organization understands and owns it.

- **Purposeful Leadership**: Leadership must be the first to promote and exemplify MTP.
- **Storytelling and communication**: Use clear stories and examples that show how MTP is applied in daily life and in the organization's actions.
- **Purpose-Centered Organizational Culture**: MTP must be present in every aspect of the culture, from hiring to day-to-day operations.

4. Incorporate MTP into the business model

For MTP to be more than just an inspiring idea, it must be embedded into the core of your business model. This means that your operations, products, and services must reflect this purpose.

- **Integrate MTP into daily operations**: Ensure every operational decision is aligned with the transformative purpose.
- **Sustainable and purposeful business models**: Develop sustainable strategies that generate both economic value and social impact.
- **Success case studies**: Get inspired by companies that have managed to integrate their MTP into their business model, keeping it as a central axis.

5. Measuring the impact of MTP

A MTP cannot remain just words. It is essential to measure its success using key performance indicators (KPIs) to evaluate its impact.

- **Essential KPIs**: Establish metrics that measure both social, environmental and cultural impact, as well as financial results.
- **Measuring non-financial impact**: Evaluate the change you are generating in society beyond traditional economic metrics.

6. Overcome resistance to change

Implementing a MTP will not be without its challenges. You are likely to encounter resistance from within and outside your organization. Here are some steps to overcome these obstacles:

- **Identify resistance to change**: Recognize areas where there is resistance and address concerns.
- **Strategies to generate buy-in**: Ensure that all levels of the organization understand the value of MTP and are involved in its implementation.
- **Overcome cultural and structural barriers**: Change the structures that oppose MTP and work on the organizational culture to align it with the purpose.

7. Scale your MTP and maximize global impact

A successful MTP doesn't stop at a local level. To maximize its impact, it's important to scale globally. Here are some key steps to achieve this:

- **Tools to scale your purpose**: Use exponential technology and platforms to expand the reach of your MTP.
- **Cases of organizations that have scaled their impact**: Learn from companies that have taken their MTP to a global level and have transformed entire industries.

8. Financing and sustainability of the MTP

Financial sustainability is key for a MTP to last over time. Here are some tips to ensure long-term financial viability:

- **How to finance your MTP**: Explore financial models including impact investing and crowdfunding.
- **Impact Investments**: Find allies who share your purpose and are willing to invest in your transformative vision.

9. Inspiration: Stories of leaders with MTP

One of the best ways to understand the value of a MTP is to learn from those who have already implemented it. Get inspired by stories of leaders who have transformed their industries and generated massive impact through their MTPs.

- **Key Lessons**: Apply these leaders' lessons to your own MTP to increase its effectiveness and scalability.

10. Building a global community around your MTP

A successful MTP is one that manages to build a global community of people who share the same mission. Here are some ways to achieve this:

- **How to create a community of support?** Engage your clients, partners and collaborators around MTP.
- **The power of global movements**: Big changes happen when people around the world unite behind a shared cause.

Conclusion

Developing and implementing a MTP requires clarity, focus, collaboration, and a long-term vision. The key steps in creating one—from identifying your core purpose to scaling your global impact—form the foundation for making your organization not just profitable, but transformative.

A well-executed MTP will not only change your organization, it will create lasting change in the world.

No. 2. Final reflection: The potential impact of a MTP on the world

Purpose **(MTP)** has the power to change not only an organization, but also the world we live in. In a global environment facing complex challenges such as climate change, social inequality, and rapid technological advancement, companies, organizations, and projects with a well-defined purpose are becoming key players in social and economic transformation.

A MTP goes beyond conventional business objectives. It is not just about making a profit or maximizing shareholder value; it is about **creating positive and lasting change** on a large scale. Those organizations that successfully implement a MTP are leading the revolution towards a more sustainable, inclusive and equitable future. The potential impact of a MTP can be measured on several levels:

1. Social and cultural transformation

A MTP has the ability to create profound changes in society. By focusing on a meaningful cause, such as inclusive education, accessible healthcare, or environmental sustainability, organizations can **catalyze social movements** that redefine human culture and behaviors. When purpose is aligned with societal needs, they become agents of change that inspire others to join and collaborate in solving global problems.

Companies with successful MTPs can influence cultural trends, foster social innovation and **lead the change agenda**. They can become role models that not only operate responsibly, but also promote new, more conscious and empathetic models of living and working.

2. Environmental impact and sustainability

The planet faces unprecedented environmental challenges. A sustainability-aligned MTP can be a transformative force in reducing the ecological footprint of organizations while inspiring others to adopt responsible practices. Companies with a clear environmental purpose—such as carbon reduction, circular economy, or resource conservation—can **help mitigate the impact of climate change** and preserve ecosystems for future generations.

The positive environmental impact that these organizations can generate goes beyond their own operations, as they can also **influence consumers and their entire value chain**, promoting sustainable practices and raising awareness about the urgent need to care for the planet.

3. Large-scale economic impact

Contrary to the belief that social and economic purposes are in conflict, well-structured MFP can be a driver of economic growth. Organizations with a clear purpose are not only more attractive to consumers, but also to investors looking for projects with social and environmental impact. The rise of impact investments and the **growing interest in socially responsible companies** demonstrates that MFP can generate strong economic returns over the long term.

Furthermore, these organizations have a greater **capacity for innovation**, as an inspiring purpose can attract top talent and foster creativity and resilience within the company. This puts them in an advantageous position to adapt to the demands of an ever-evolving market.

4. Inspiration and global mobilization

One of the most powerful effects of a MTP is its ability to **inspire and mobilize people around the world**. When an organization articulates a clear, transformative purpose, it becomes a beacon of hope that lights the way for others. This kind of inspiration not only attracts customers and collaborators, but also generates global movements that connect individuals and organizations around a common cause.

Through the power of social media, technology and global collaboration, the impact of a MTP can **be exponentially amplified**, mobilizing resources, people and ideas in ways never before possible. Companies that embrace a global purpose position themselves as leaders on the international stage and create engaged communities that seek to create systemic change.

5. Leadership towards a resilient future

Finally, organizations with a clear MTP are better prepared to face the challenges of the future. In an increasingly uncertain and changing world, transformative purposes provide **a moral and strategic compass** that allows companies to stay focused on their mission, even in times of crisis. By having a greater cause guiding them, these organizations are more resilient, innovative, and able to adapt to changes in the environment.

The MTP acts as a **reference point** for long-term decision making, ensuring that the company does not lose sight of its large-scale impact, even in the most difficult times.

Final reflection

The potential impact of a MTP on the world is limitless. A transformative purpose not only has the power to change an organization, but it can also mobilize millions of people to act for a better future. At a historic moment when the world needs bold, innovative and scalable solutions, MTPs are becoming the most powerful tools to face global challenges. Organizations that embrace this philosophy and act with purpose will not only lead the future, but **will be the drivers of global transformation**.

The impact of a MTP transcends borders and sectors. By developing and adopting one, you will not only be improving your organization, but contributing to a significant change in the world. It is a commitment to the future, to future generations, and to the possibility of building a more just, equitable, and sustainable world.

#3 Final Summary: Call to action: How to start your transformative journey today?

The concept of **Massive Transformative Purpose (MTP)** is more than just an inspiring idea. It is an invitation to **take action** and begin a journey that will not only impact your organization, but will also contribute to improving the world. However, that journey begins with a decision: to commit to a bigger purpose, dare to dream big, and put in place the actions necessary to make it a reality.

Below is a call to action with concrete steps that you can begin implementing **today** to take the first steps toward a transformative purpose:

1. Reflect on the core purpose of your organization

The first step toward a MTP begins with a deep **internal reflection** on your organization's values and mission. Ask yourself:

- Why does my organization exist beyond profit?
- What positive impact do I want to make in the world?
- How can I improve people's lives and contribute to solving global problems?

Take the time to meet with your leadership team and discuss these issues. This exercise will allow you **to identify the foundations** on which your MTP will be built. Even if your current mission is not completely clear, this is the ideal time to recalibrate it and align it with a more transformative purpose.

Immediate Action: Schedule a meeting with your key team to discuss your organization's core values and how you could make them more ambitious and impactful.

2. Involve your team in the MTP definition process

A MTP isn't created alone. You need commitment and input from all levels of the organization to ensure the purpose is authentic and resonant. Involving your team in this process not only creates a sense of ownership, but also offers a diverse perspective on the challenges you can tackle as a collective.

Organize workshops or **collaborative brainstorming sessions** so that all members of your organization can contribute their ideas and experiences. This process will not only enrich the purpose, but will also foster a greater connection with the company's mission.

Immediate action: Create a teamwork dynamic to start brainstorming about the MTP, where everyone can contribute with their vision on the impact that the organization should have.

3. Define ambitious and scalable goals

A MTP must be ambitious enough to impact millions of people. Once you have defined the core purpose, it is essential to set **concrete objectives** that are scalable and that allow you to take your vision beyond the local or regional scope.

These goals don't have to be achieved immediately, but they should serve as a **clear guide** for where your organization is headed and how it plans to amplify its impact.

Immediate action: Review your current goals and assess how you could make them more ambitious and expansive to create change on a larger scale. Consider what additional resources you would need to reach more people.

4. Integrate MTP into your business model

For a MTP to be effective, it must not simply be a slogan or an inspirational phrase. It must be **integrated into every aspect** of your business model, from product development to the way you interact with your customers. Align your operational processes, marketing strategies, and investment decisions with the transformative purpose you have defined.

Immediate action: Identify at least one area of your business model or operation where you can begin to implement changes that reflect your MTP. This can be something as simple as changing the focus of a product or service so that it is more aligned with your values.

5. Communicate your MTP in a clear and exciting way

Once you've defined your MTP, the next step is **to communicate it to the world** effectively. This is where the power of storytelling plays a crucial role. Create a compelling narrative that not only explains what your purpose is, but also inspires others to join your cause.

Your communication should be clear, emotive and aspirational. You're not just selling a product or service; you're sharing a vision for the future. The goal is **to connect emotionally** with your employees, customers and the community at large to create a movement around your purpose.

Immediate action: Develop an initial narrative for your MTP that you can share on your communication channels (website, social media, internal presentations). Make sure it is inspiring and accessible.

6. Create a long-term action plan and commitment

A MTP is not a goal that is achieved overnight. It requires commitment and a **clear action plan** that guides your organization toward implementing and scaling the purpose over the long term. Define key milestones and metrics that allow you to measure progress toward your purpose and adjust course when necessary.

This long-term commitment must include clear financing and sustainability strategies, ensuring that the CFP can endure over time and adapt to changing circumstances.

Immediate Action: Establish a short, medium, and long-term plan to achieve your MTP milestones. Break this plan down into actionable steps and assign responsibilities to each team member.

7. Foster a purpose-based organizational culture

For your MTP to truly transform your organization, it is crucial that **everyone** in the company, from leaders to the newest employees, is aligned with the purpose. Fostering a purpose-based organizational culture means that every decision, behavior, and daily practice must be oriented toward the transformative mission.

An organization with a strong culture around MTP not only generates a positive impact on the world, but also attracts and retains talent that shares the same vision for change.

Immediate action: Review your organizational culture and adjust internal practices to align with your purpose. This may include changing the approach to performance reviews, the way purpose is communicated in meetings, and how goal achievement is celebrated.

8. Connect with a global community and strategic allies

A MTP cannot be achieved alone. You need **strategic alliances** and a global community that supports and amplifies your purpose. Seek to collaborate with other organizations, NGOs, governments, and global movements that share your mission. By connecting with a larger network, you can scale your impact and accelerate change.

Additionally, a supportive global community will provide you with resources, knowledge and greater reach, making it easier to implement your MTP in different contexts.

Immediate Action: Research organizations and allies that share a similar purpose and begin making connections that can lead to future collaborations.

9. Act today: The first step is decisive

The journey toward **Massive Transformative Purpose** can seem daunting at first, but the key is **to start today**. You don't need to have everything figured out to take action. Every small step you take in the right direction will bring you closer to a future where your organization is not only successful, but transformative.

Remember, change doesn't happen overnight, but every action counts. The sooner you start moving toward your MTP, the faster you'll start seeing results. The important thing is to commit to the process, be consistent, and adjust course when necessary.

Final Summary

This is your call to action. **The world needs more organizations with a MTP** – companies that go beyond the conventional to generate a positive and lasting impact. Today you have the opportunity to be part of that change. No matter how big or small your organization is, your purpose has the potential to transform lives, communities and the entire world.

Start your transformative journey **today**. Define your purpose, align your team, and act with intention. The future belongs to those who dare to lead with purpose, and you are one step away from being one of those leaders.

Businessman, entrepreneur, visionary, leader, ...ready to start?

What do you need to perform a MTP?

Come on, let's get started! Creating a **Massive Transformative Purpose (MTP)** is a big step. It's not just a nice phrase or a vision of what you'd like your company to be; it's a real commitment to something bigger than your business, something that will have a positive impact on the world. But what exactly do you need to achieve it? Let's break it down in a clear and practical way:

1. A clear and profound reason for being

First and foremost, you need to have a genuine purpose that goes beyond profit. Ask yourself: **Why does your company exist? What big problem do you want to solve?**

It's not just about selling a product or service; it's about thinking about how your business can improve people's lives or contribute to solving a global problem. If you can find that deeper reason for being, you already have the foundation of your MTP.

Example: If you have a food company, your MVP should not just be "selling food" but something like **"eradicating child malnutrition in your country"**. It is an ambitious, big goal, but achievable with a good plan.

2. A long-term vision

A MTP isn't something you achieve in a year or two. **It's a long-term goal**, an ambitious target that will likely take time to achieve. You need to be able to look beyond the immediate successes and think about how your business can evolve to meet that goal in the future.

This type of vision requires patience and perseverance. You'll have to **resist the temptation of quick wins** if they don't align with your purpose. The key is to stay true to your vision, even when the road seems difficult.

3. Emotional connection with your team and your clients

For a MTP to be successful, **your team and your customers need to believe in it as much as you do**. It's not enough for you as a leader to have a clear purpose; you need others to share it, too. This is achieved by creating a company culture where **everyone feels part of something bigger**.

Communication is key here. Use stories, examples, and experiences to convey why this purpose is important. Tell your employees how their work contributes to MTP and show your customers how your business positively impacts their lives or the world.

Example: If your MTP is to reduce plastic pollution, involve your team in green initiatives within the company. Make it possible for customers to participate too, such as by purchasing products with sustainable packaging.

4. Adaptability

The world is changing rapidly, and your MTP must be flexible enough to **adapt to those changes**. While the core purpose remains the same, the strategies to achieve it must evolve over time. Stay open to new ideas, technologies, and approaches that help you accomplish your mission.

Don't be afraid to make adjustments as you go. The important thing is that even though the means may change, **the heart of your purpose remains intact**.

5. Commitment to action

MTP isn't just pretty words on a piece of paper or a web page; it requires **consistent action**. This involves making changes to your business that support your purpose and making decisions that keep it at the center of your strategy.

Make it part of your **daily operations**, from the type of products you offer to the initiatives you support as a company. Every small step should bring you closer to fulfilling that big purpose.

Example: If your MTP is to improve education in rural areas, you could commit to donating a percentage of your income to schools in remote areas or create mentoring programs for underprivileged students.

6. Strategic collaborations

No one can change the world alone. A MTP often requires **partnerships** with other organizations, companies or individuals who share your values and goals. Find **strategic partners** who can help you achieve the transformative change you are looking for.

It's not just about business partnerships. These can be **nonprofits, governments, or local communities** that are working toward the same goal. Collaborating with others will allow you to amplify the impact of your MTP.

7. A mindset of resilience

Finally, you will need **resilience**. The path to making a MTP will not be easy or quick. There will be obstacles, times when things don't go as planned, and difficult decisions to make. The important thing is **to not give up** and stay true to your purpose, knowing that the fruits of your effort will come in time.

Think of transformational purpose as a big mountain you're climbing. Sometimes the climb will be tough, but the view from the top – when you see the positive impact you've created – will be worth it.

Creating a MTP isn't an instant process, but if you commit to your purpose and follow these steps, you can turn your company into a **transformative force in the world**. The key is to have clarity, perseverance, and a strong connection with the people around you.

www.ingramcontent.com/pod-product-compliance
Lightning Source LLC
Chambersburg PA
CBHW062111220526
45471CB00010B/3692